Between Two Worlds
East and West

Professor J.N. Mohanty

Between Two Worlds
East and West

An Autobiography

J.N. Mohanty

OXFORD
UNIVERSITY PRESS

OXFORD
UNIVERSITY PRESS

YMCA Library Building, Jai Singh Road, New Delhi 110 001

Oxford University Press is a department of the University of Oxford. It furthers the
University's objective of excellence in research, scholarship, and education
by publishing worldwide in

Oxford   New York

Auckland   Bangkok   Buenos Aires   Cape Town   Chennai
Dar es Salaam   Delhi   Hong Kong   Istanbul   Karachi   Kolkata
Kuala Lumpur   Madrid   Melbourne   Mexico City   Mumbai   Nairobi
São Paulo   Shanghai   Singapore   Taipei   Tokyo   Toronto

with an associated company in Berlin

Published in India
By Oxford University Press, New Delhi

First published 2002

ISBN 019 564 8358

Typeset in Times New Roman 10.5/12
By Jojy Philip
Printed by Roopak Printers, Delhi 110 032
Published by Manzar Khan, Oxford University Press
YMCA Library Building, Jai Singh Road, New Delhi 110 001

In remembrance of my aunt Rama Devi Chowdhury
who showed, but did not say,
how life can be good, beautiful, and holy.

Contents

Foreword

This is the life story of an Indian philosopher who has spent his life in three countries: India, Germany, and the USA.

The writing has gone through many phases. Large parts were written in Germany and in Calcutta. I am sending it to press almost fifteen years after I began writing. One thing I did not want to do was write another book on philosophy, or even an account of my philosophy. However, since my life has been primarily dedicated to the pursuit of philosophical ideas, the connection of the story of my life to my philosophical interests was almost unavoidable. It was equally important for me to retrieve my 'origin', my 'roots' in my village in Orissa, India. Calcutta and Göttingen have been recurrent presences in between, shaping my mind and spirit.

Kenneth Merrill patiently read the penultimate draft of this book. His unfailing sense of the English language and his sympathetic *Verstehen* of my life helped remove many of my linguistic infelicities and lapses. Without the help of Bina Gupta, this book could not have been published. Bina Gupta improved the story with her sensitive responses; but for her willingness to prepare the final draft, the book would not have been published.

I present here a story of how one person, Indian by birth and upbringing, Hindu by faith, philosopher by profession, living in the USA for three decades, thankful to the country of adoption but never forgetting the Indian heritage, has responded to the world at large and interpreted his life. Remembrance and interpretation have mingled—this story is a response to history.

J.N.M.

The Town and the Village

The city of Cuttack then had red, dusty roads. Old brick houses, some with roofs and some thatched, stood along them, interspersed with slums of mud huts and bamboo-walled shacks. The town lies encircled by two mighty rivers, the one a tributary of the other, enclosed as it were in an age-old conspiracy not to let the town grow beyond the limits imposed by them. In summer and in winter, the rivers are but vast expanses of sand with tiny trickling streams in one, and a larger expanse of deep blue water in the other, protected and held together by a crumbling dam that had been built nearly a century ago by the British. The monsoons transform the rivers into mighty torrents of water that sweep past the city, washing down trees and mud huts, cattle, even elephants, living creatures and corpses, human and animal. Old Oriya kings who made Cuttack their capital built enormous stone embankments on both the sides of the city to protect it from the wrath of the waters. There is no doubt that but for their farsighted work, the two rivers would by now, have been flowing on one bed, and the city of Cuttack reduced to their sands. However, the city stands—an age-old relic to days gone, saved from destruction but closed in by space and time.

To grow up in such a place as Cuttack is to feel secure that nothing will matter in the long run. Perhaps the only fear I experienced as a boy of ten was watching the fury and wrath of the waters of the Kāthjori, on whose banks we lived, in spate. But this fear would soon subside, with the thought that this was an annual show of futile wrath, as the very existence of the city tells us so convincingly. The ruins of the fort on the north side of the city on the banks of the Mahānadī—a fort which reportedly was nine-storeys high but of which a shapeless brick mound, a moat and a stately gateway are all that remain—were supposed to fill the mind of every Oriya child with a sense of pride in the greatness of the people who spoke her tongue. As a young boy, that sense of pride filled my entire being. But then life went on, chiefly around the families that were related by ties of marriage and friendship. I found myself to be a point within a series of concentric circles, the innermost circle of which was my family—my parents and my siblings. But the line of demarcation between these families was rather thin. A family was not bound by rigid and impenetrable walls, nor by strict definitions. Often the neighbour, a friend or a distant relative would acquire the privilege of being an insider, an 'uncle', a 'brother', or a 'sister'. My people carried this flexibility from their villages to the towns.

A long stretch of dusty, red road began at a railroad station on the other side of the river Mahānadī, the great river, the larger of the two that enclose Cuttack between them. The road wound first through mounds of white sand deposited by the wind from the enormous expanse of the river's bed, but then ran through fertile rice fields bound on both sides by a densely set wall of mango, banyan and coconut palms, through which the clusters of mud huts of the villages were barely visible. There were little ponds by the roadside with white lilies and red lotuses on their waters. To the young observer, bamboo groves presented fearful images of deadly snakes. The wide-ranging arms of the banyan trees appeared as the habitat of invisible and mischievous spirits of all sizes and descriptions. Every few miles, a half-ton bus would come to a stop at a tiny roadside village, usually—if it were a mail bus—to pick up and unload the mail bag, but also to load and unload passengers and their baggage from the roof. Besides the post office (marked by a red post-box sticking to the mud wall of a one-room mud hut), there would be a cluster of tea shops and eating places (where food is served on lotus leaves on rows of dark wooden tables, which, after eating, you throw into an outdoor garbage dump to the excitement and delight of a couple of the canine species who kept vigil around the place). After several such road-side stops, which included one or two relatively larger townships, the weary bus would pull into a tiny cluster of mud huts among which a red-white brick Public Works Department bungalow stood out with remarkable pride and pre-eminence. The family would disembark, luggage pulled down from the roof top, curious village urchins would gather in excitement, the village elders who knew us would bow down to my father—once a boy from a nearby village, who had made it big in the town as a lawyer and then as a judge; then there would begin, in a row of bullock carts, a journey along a muddy road demarcated by rows of date palms from the vast stretch of rice fields on both sides. We youngsters would marvel at the skill of the cart drivers in negotiating the carts along the terrain, as also at their strength and courage in commanding and being obeyed by those stout bullocks whose long horns were always threatening us. In the summer, the road would be hardened with mud, the carts would bump; in the rainy season, the muddy path would be indistinguishable from the sheet of water all around, but for the rows of palms and the winding open space between the tall rice plants, and if the bullocks were not able to pull the carts through, there would be servants, or even passers-by, who would lend their hands to push them across a ditch.

The village of Nilakaṇṭhapur (the seat of the blue-necked god, i.e., Śiva) is part of a chain of villages that merge into each other. Although these villages are not physically separate from each other, they are distinct legal entities, and perhaps have their distinct social personalities. At one end of Nilakaṇṭhapur, where the complex chain of villages may be said to begin, as it were, where the main street emerges out of the village green (a patch of common green bound by hedges of *kiyā*, shaded by several massive banyans that stand witness to the funeral pyres that have been lighted at one end of the field bordering the hedge, while at the other end boys play native games or swing on the branches of the trees, and cows graze), there stands the house which I learnt to identify emotionally as 'ours'. Though I was born in the city of Cuttack, and raised wherever my father was posted (the administration required that judges could serve at one station at most for three years). Every vacation brought us back to this home.

The home was in fact a cluster of homes; the family consisted of many families. One side of a large square was taken up by a row of houses, each of which had a hallway opening into the common square in front. Then there was a first inner courtyard, around which there were living rooms, and behind it a second inner courtyard, around which there were kitchens, pantries and storerooms, all of these again leading to a large tank which supplied water for most household work. Each of these homes belonged to a 'branch' of a family which originally must have been one, but now the branches represent different places in a complex family tree, and not all connections between all of them are known totmany. There was, however, a shared sense of belonging; joys and sorrows were shared, weddings and births were celebrated, deaths were mourned in common. Each, however, was a distinct legal entity. Some were moderately wealthy, others nearly paupers; some then owned lots of land, others none at all.

On one side of the common square and adjoining one end of the row of homes, there was the cattle shed, which was divided up into spaces for the different families. On the side opposite the cattle shed stood the barn house, where once paddy was stored for all, but which, as everything else, had been divided and subdivided into many different storage rooms. No family would move into a new homestead. This was the ancestral plot. The remaining side of the square was taken up by the family temple. Some one hundred and fifty years ago, an ancestor, Chaturbhuja by name, went on pilgrimage by foot to Vrindāvan, about a thousand miles away, and returned home carrying two idols, one of Kṛṣṇa and the other of Rādhā, the former in black *muguni* stone, the latter in bronze. Since then all the branches of the family worship these idols, share in performing the ceremonies and rituals, and take care of the temple premises. Old men retire into the temple's outbuildings. Children learn their lessons on the temple verandah. Family guests live there. Unexpected guests sleep on the outer verandah and do not go unfed. Kṛṣṇa's *prasādam* is always available. In the evening, the ladies send flower garlands that they painstakingly put together during the afternoon. When the evening sets in and the cattle have returned home, the priest performs the *ārati*, the old and the young—in dwindling numbers these days, for the old are dying and the young are leaving for the towns—sing *kīrtan* in chorus to the accompaniment of *mrdang* and *kartāla*. Without the temple, there would be no centre of gravity in the lives of those people, no space beyond the cramped space of living, and no moment outside of the time filled with work, to step outside for a glimpse into the transcendent: into life beyond and things not quite understood.

When we came home, there was no space for so many visitors within the old family dwelling. The ladies and girls found a room, but the men, old and young, shared the outer houses around the temple. I felt secure from the snakes (I imagined them to be there) and spirits—none of these evil ones dared enter the temple precincts. We boys would sleep on a palm-leaf mat on the temple verandah; we were warned not to sleep in front of the main temple door, for quite a few old men and women had glimpses of the deity Kṛṣṇa slipping out of the temple at the dead of night, on horseback, when all eyes—save those of the lucky witnesses—were closed in sleep.

School and College

I never studied in the village school. There was a one-room 'lower primary' school to which in the early hours of the morning, after the cattle had gone out to graze, little boys and girls made their way, with tiny square palm-leaf mats on one hand and dark slates framed in wood on the other. Here they learnt reading, writing and (mental) arithmetic. The 'upper primary' and 'minor' schools were larger establishments, with teachers for each class, a Headmaster for each school, and an apology of a playground. Students read aloud, learnt the numerical tables by reciting them together; there was a continuous humming that broke the stillness of the village centre. Boys and girls, wealthy or pauper, joined under these roofs, and formed an acquaintance that, I always thought, nothing later on could diminish. My father, who had 'made it' in the town recalled with emotion and affection his boyhood friends—the village carpenter, the blacksmith, the temple priest and many others—who would, when he was in the village, congregate around him after it was dark; they had nothing else to do but converse endlessly.

Into that community of hearts I never really entered. Since my father came to the village only during vacations, and spent the rest of the year in the town, my brothers and sisters and I went to the government English schools in the town. The government schools were invariably sturdier brick buildings, not mud huts; they had spacious playgrounds where we played soccer. I have been told that I began to speak rather late; that my first lessons in the alphabet were from the family cook; that when my brother, just a little older than I, was first sent to school, I cried and cried, for I felt that too should have gone to the school with him. And so I did go to school, ill-prepared, with poor skills in reading and writing. However, I survived the early embarrassment and very soon caught up with the rest of the class.

Those were the last years of the British Raj in India. Eleven years after I started school (at the age of eight), India was divided in order to be free. But as this school-going boy surveyed the world around him, he did not have the slightest premonition of the end of the mighty empire. The Raj appeared to be still secure. In the living rooms of the English-educated middle class, in classrooms and post offices, railroad stations and roadside tea shops—the King's portrait smiled benignly at us. We were taught in English, but did not have any British teachers as my father's generation had. My mother tongue, Oriya, was taught as a vernacular—that is how the class schedule put it. Sanskrit, Arabic, and Persian were classics from among which one had to choose one in the higher forms. As I look back, I recall some of my teachers with the fondest memories. They were not only good teachers, but taught with genuine sincerity and authority. There were indeed two sets of instructors: in school and at home. Private tutors supplemented and reinforced what was covered in school. They taught either in the morning hours before school started, or in the evening hours after we returned from the playground. They were either teachers in the very school we went to, or perhaps office clerks with a B.A. degree. Invariably, they knew their English—spelling and grammar—well, and their mathematics straight.

Some remarkable personalities stand out even now. There was the Sanskrit teacher, the *pandit*, Nilakantha Misra, who taught me (as well as my brother and older sister) Sanskrit at home. Every morning three of us would recite conjugations and declensions of Sanskrit verbs and nouns loud enough to be heard outside the house; we would compete to do it first. The *pandit* taught me all the grammar that I learnt later. He also taught this ten-year-old boy the primer of logic *Tarkasaṃgraha*, and Kalidāsa's *Raghuvaṃśam*. Love of Sanskrit remained indelibly imprinted on my mind. There was also the mathematics teacher, Srinatha Roy, who once advised me: 'Jitendra, walk barefoot, contact with the earth will energize your brain.' Then there was the English teacher who drilled into me the notion that to spell incorrectly was 'ungentlemanly'; the private tutor for mathematics who wanted me not merely to solve problems, but to solve them most elegantly; another who first told me, when I was in class seven, that Sarvapalli Radhakrishnan, the Indian philosopher (later to be India's president) was 'a genius' (we were talking, I suppose, about what the word 'genius' meant). And school, whether in the small town of Bhadrak on the encircling river Salandi, or in Cuttack, the capital city of the state, was invigorating and enriching. We played soccer at school and badminton at home during the winter. The three most exciting days in the school year, to which we looked forward, were the annual sports day, the prize distribution day (when I invariably received loads of book prizes for academic achievements), and the day on which we worshipped Saraswati, the goddess of learning, which incidentally was the only religious day observed in the school. The evening before the festival, we would decorate a room, hang coloured festoons and garlands, set up a stage for the goddess—a beautiful woman, clad in white, with a *veenā* in one hand and books in the other, a lovely swan at her feet. We would keep our books by her side, to be blessed by her. Early in the morning, we would go around town, stealing flowers from gardens, weave them into garlands for the goddess, after which the priest would take over. The festival—on which we would be given new clothes to wear—symbolized the arrival of spring. Mango leaves and buds of mangoes would be all around us, and birds would start to sing after winter. A new crop of vegetables—cabbage, peas, eggplant and tomatoes—would be cooked into a marvellous curry for the occasion. Music would fill the air in the evening. Our young hearts would pine for something, we knew not what, something beyond studies, beyond the confines of our homes, perhaps for the ethereal touch of something sweet and delicate. Life was changing.

It was in Cuttack, in my senior year—1942, it was—that something violent, but no less intoxicating, entered life, both at home and in school. The previous year, Gandhi had asked that his followers 'violate' the law (of the British rulers) and court imprisonment. My two uncles and their wives (in whose care my elder brother and I had been left by our parents, in order to study in Cuttack's most famous school)—Gopabandhu Chaudhury and Rama Devi, Nabakrushna Chaudhury and Malati Devi—went to jail, following the Mahatma. But that was for a short period of time. Some negotiations in Delhi led to their release, and they returned home with stories of their adventures in the jails. We felt proud of them and wished we had been there. But that freedom did not last long. On 8 August 1942, Gandhi asked the British to 'quit India', courted arrest in Bombay, and so did his leading followers around the country. The country was on fire, so were our young hearts. My elder uncle and aunt, being more staunch Gandhians, 'courted' imprisonment. The younger couple, at heart Marxist 'revolutionaries', went 'underground', pursued by the police. How proud we were of them! Detectives kept their vigilant eyes on the house, and we would give them the impression that the two were 'inside' the house; the police would search in vain, and we would heartily enjoy their frustration. Politics entered the school. Our elders, my father and the school's headmaster, silently conveyed their sympathy for the Gandhian movement, but advised us to attend to our studies and not to do anything foolish—for, they told us, the country, when independent, would be in dire need of educated people to run it. And so we did what they told us to do.

In the final matriculation examination, I stood first in Orissa, and enrolled myself in Ravenshaw College in Cuttack. The college consisted of a set of modern buildings with well-kept quadrangles inside, two large hostels for students on both sides (and was admired by us for imitating Oxbridge). What excitement it was to bicycle from the house at one end of the town to college at the other end, a distance of about three miles, and to be a college student at last. I studied Mathematics, Logic and Sanskrit, and the two compulsory subjects, English and Oriya (my mother tongue). The college library was the first library I learned to use. I would borrow heaps of books to read. One of the things I promised myself was that I would read the main works of Nobel Prize-winning authors. I read Anatole France, Andre Gide, Thomas Mann, Knut Hamsun, Sigried Undset, Henrik Ibsen, George Bernard Shaw and Rabindranath Tagore, among others. I also borrowed a copy of Kant's *Critique of Pure Reason*, tried to read large parts of it and made my notes, but am afraid I did not understand much. It was at this time that my high school friend, Aboni Ghose, introduced me to the writings of Sri Aurobindo. Aboni (who had begun to spell his name 'Aubony') had already grown a full beard and wore his hair long at the back; we all took for granted that he was practising Yoga. He had already published an Oriya translation of a small booklet by Sri Aurobindo on Yoga, had a large collection in his home of Sri Aurobindo's books, and knew many of his disciples. He made me read Sri Aurobindo's magnum opus, *Life Divine*. I read perhaps the first six chapters, which impressed me a great deal by their profundity and large scope. I even made plans to write a book on metaphysics myself, with chapters on 'matter', 'life', 'mind', and so forth. Soon after joining college, Aubony and I started a study circle at the residence of a friend, Kangali Pati (who later joined the Aurobindo Ashram in Pondicherry, changed his name to 'Prapatti', and succeeded, in the sixties and seventies, in spreading Sri Aurobindo's message throughout Orissa). Kangali lived in a thatched one-room mud hut. Besides the three of us, was an economist, an Oriya poet, and some others, whose names I do not now recall, met in his room once a week to read and discuss the writings of Aurobindo, Vivekananda and Gandhi. I am not sure if I also tried Yoga, although I may have at times sat down with eyes closed and tried to think of 'nothing'.

In college, I became active in the debating society. I would write down a speech, learn it by heart, and alone, on the roof of our house, deliver the speech aloud. Gradually, I became quite good, and won all the prizes and medals the college had to offer for debating. After going to Calcutta, I gave up debating; my fellow students—Mohit Sen and Shibendu Ghose—were better speakers than I was.

At last, the two years of college in Cuttack were over, I took the 'Intermediate Arts' examinations and stood first in the University. The boy who stood third, Janaki Patnaik, went on to become the Chief Minister of Orissa for quite some time, and the boy who stood tenth, Ranganath Misra, recently retired as the Chief Justice of the Supreme Court of India. My future lay elsewhere. 'Now', my father said, 'you must go outside the state to face greater competition'. A friend of my father suggested that I should try the Presidency College in Calcutta. With letters of introduction to many people at Presidency, at the end of June in 1945, I boarded a Calcutta-bound train, full of soldiers returning from the Burma front.

The Family

Most families in Cuttack maintained their village roots, as did my father, Jagannath Mohanty. Educated at the local village school, the local college in Cuttack, and finally the University of Calcutta (where he got a First Class in Economics, and then in Law), he had lost his parents in his early childhood, and was raised by uncles and aunts. True to the spirit of traditional joint families, he was never treated like an orphan. The uncle who headed the family raised my father like his own son, and in no way favoured his own children over him. Back from Calcutta, my father started a law practice in Cuttack under Swami Bichitrananda Das (who was called 'Swamiji' because of his saintly disposition). The latter had been trained under Orissa's most famous lawyer-politician-social activist, the first Oriya Barrister, as a matter of fact the first Oriya to have gone West, Madhusudana Das. I mention this, for it was this connection that led to my mother's marriage with my father.

My mother's family was more urban. Her father, Gokulananda Chaudhury, had established himself in the town of Cuttack as a very successful lawyer, who had accumulated a lot of wealth, built a large home , lived a life of luxury and also aspired to political leadership. His political rival was Madhusudana Das. The political platform in Cuttack, in the first decade of the twentieth century, consisted mainly of the autonomy of India within the British empire, and the creation of Orissa as a separate state (within India), so that educated Oriyas could get more opportunities for the advancement of their careers. The Indian National Congress had not till that time declared political independence for India as its goal. Orissa, along with Bihar, was a part of the larger state of Bengal, in which Bengalis, already advanced in English education, enjoyed preferences and privileges. The Oriyas were proud that Orissa was the last province to fall into British hands, while Bengal was the first; but this was also responsible for Bengal's advancement in respect of English education, which gave rise to a powerful, sophisticated class of English-educated, often knighted, professional middle class, which spread out over the rest of India as the local bureaucratic wing of the Raj. Gokulananda Choudhury, along with Madhusudana Das, represented the resentment as well as the aspiration of the Oriyas at the court of the British.

The families of the two also entered into matrimonial alliance. Madhu Babu's younger brother's daughter, Rama, was given in marriage to Gokulananda's eldest son, Gopabandhu; the mediator between the two families was one Raj Kisore Das, who was a middle-level official in English officialdom (the highest rank that the Oriyas achieved at the time in the bureaucracy). A leader of the *karaṇa* caste in the town, he was already related to Madhu Babu's family by marriage—he was a maternal uncle of the bride and also a friend of the Chaudhury family. My father's only sister was the wife of this Raj Kisore Das's brother. It is out of this complex net of inter-family relations, that my father—a promising lawyer, coming from the landed gentry—was chosen as the groom for Gokulananda's youngest daughter, Basanta Kumari (by which time Gokulananda was already dead from a stroke preceded by excessive drinking).

My mother was the youngest of five surviving children: two brothers and two sisters (one of whom we learnt much later was adopted, but that made no difference to her position as the eldest child of the family). The two brothers were Gopabandhu and Nabakrusna. Gopabandhu went to Calcutta to study mathematics at the Presidency College, and lived in the Eden Hindu Hostel (a path I would follow much later). A bright and intelligent young man, he was noted for his life of luxury, love of food and friends, and *āddā* (that almost untranslatable Bengali word for endless light conversation). Out of college, he entered the British Civil Service, and served a few years as a Deputy District Collector (a powerful position for an Oriya to occupy at that time). It has often happened that an utterly contingent event changes the direction and meaning of a person's life. This happened to Gopabandhu. When he was posted at Jajpur—a rural town in the district of Cuttack—the surrounding countryside was flooded by rivers, all tributaries of the Mahanadi, in spate. As the administrative official in charge, he reported the situation to the British administrators higher up, but was asked to keep quiet. The human misery around him was too much for him to keep quiet about, and he resigned from the civil service in protest. The family wealth, after his father's death, had declined, but persistent as he was, he had made up his mind. His young wife, Rama, gave her consent. They started a life of unflinching and selfless service to the poor and downtrodden in Orissa. In 1921, Gandhi came to Orissa and asked for donations for the cause of the *Harijans* or untouchables, 'the children of God' as he called the untouchables. Rama took all her jewellery—an enormous amount of gold that she had been given by her wealthy parents and in-laws at her wedding—and put the bag in the Mahatma's hands. An irrevocable decision had been made.

My mother's younger brother, Nabakrusna, was in college. Following his elder brother, he gave up college, met Gandhi, spent some time in the Mahatma's Ashram at Sabarmati, and eventually landed in Santiniketan, the school and the Ashram founded by the Nobel Prize-winning Bengali poet Rabindranath Tagore. I do not know if he enrolled in any course, but he certainly pursued his wide-ranging intellectual interests. I can imagine that he was an introvert like me, engaged with his own thoughts, trying to put Gandhi, Marx and Tagore together (but it was Marx who won, initially), and dreaming of a social revolution in Orissa. It was there that he fell in love with a brilliant Bengali girl, Malati Sen, who had learnt singing and acting from the poet himself, and who took part in dance-dramas that the poet wrote and first produced at Santiniketan. Their marriage—she being a Brahmo[1]—shocked the *karana* community in Cuttack (as mine did nearly thirty years later); but it was his elder brother's wife, Rama Devi, and my mother who gave Malati Sen, fondly called Minu, protection and moral support when my grandmother, already widowed, would not even let her serve food and drink or enter her kitchen. The two, Nabakrusna and Malati, complemented each other: his introverted and intellectual nature was balanced by her dynamic social activism, his political culture by her aestheticism. Both led political movements, founded the peasants' movement in Orissa against the landlords, and led movements, often violent, of the people against the Rājās and Mahārājās, who still ruled with absolute power in certain parts of Orissa. Malati continued to sing all the while.

These two couples—Gopabandhu and Rama Chaudhury, Nabakrusna and Malati Chaudhury—had the greatest influence on me during my youth. Through them, Gandhi ceased to be a distant reality (as Nicolai Hartmann would have said, not a mere 'ought to do', but rather a positive 'ought-to-be'), and the ideals of social justice (and the challenge of

---

[1] Not synonymous with '*Brahmin*', but stands for a new reform movement within Hinduism, founded in the 19th century.

working towards it) became an incarnate actuality. All four represented very different person-types. Gopabandhu was a man of action: for him, once a course of action was recognized as an ought-to-do, there was no hesitation in executing it, no intellectual exercise was needed either to justify it, to cast doubt on it—you simply had to do it, or try your best to do it, until you died. He seldom discussed intellectual ideas. Only once did he write to me, when I was just finishing my doctorate in Germany, that, in his view, Vinoba Bhave—Gandhi's disciple about whom I will speak later—had enriched the value of philosophy, for he had shown, or rather was showing how philosophy can be practically effective. Instead of saying, as I was afraid he would say, that philosophy was useless, he wanted to say—like the so-called Hegelians of the left—that philosophy had to be 'realized', and that Vinoba was doing just that. Although he had enormous affection for me, and he would affectionately refer to me as 'the philosopher', I think he realized in his heart of hearts that I was doing something important, something intrinsically good, and also that his own path, the path of action, was different, and time was short (both the time left for him, as well as the demands of the goal he was working towards), so he had better work unceasingly to achieve that goal. For his co-workers, he had affection, but affection was tempered by sternness, that he thought 'walking on the razor's edge' required: no compromise with deviations. He would not censure or punish (for how could he, he had no power?); he would go his own way. Sometimes, when this uncompromising sternness caused pain to others, he would surprisingly come back to smoothen and comfort with good humour, without compromising at the fundamental level.

Here are two examples of his responses. Once, when I was living in the Hardinge Hostel of Calcutta University, he came to the city, and stopped by to see me. I was in college, so he waited for me in my room (which was opened for him by the floor servant, who knew of his relationship to me). He waited for some time, and finding me late in returning, left—leaving the following note on my desk: 'Sorry I missed you. Found on your desk a pile of old letters including some written by me. A philosopher should not save, that makes you cling to the past instead of being free for the future. Cultivate non-attachment'. I destroyed the letters. If some of them were here, I would have now reconstructed my story much better.

The other incident took place during the wedding of his younger brother Nabakrusna's daughter, Uttara. Uttara, or Bubu as she was called, was a few months older than me, and we grew up as close friends. She was marrying Narayan Desai, the only son of the late Mahadev

Desai, Gandhi's life-long private secretary. Nabakrusna Chaudhury was at the time the Chief Minister of Orissa. The official residence of the Chief Minister was decorated and illuminated by multicoloured lights. People from all parts of Orissa (and India) came with gifts for the bride and bridegroom. A large room was filled with gifts. Just before the wedding was to begin, Gopabandhu arrived. When he saw the pomp and splendour and the gifts, he quietly called his brother aside and wanted all the gifts to be returned before he could participate in the wedding ceremony. 'We did not sacrifice all we had', he said, 'to enjoy the benefits of independence *for ourselves*'. His voice quivered with anger. His instructions were followed; all the gifts returned, and the wedding began with the austerity that marked all Gandhian celebrations.

With that unflinching dedication to his ideals—he had said a similar thing when after India's independence, he was asked by Nehru if he would consent to be the Governor of the state, and also when Utkal University was considering a proposal to confer an honorary doctorate on him—the end came, almost inevitably, in disappointment. He had been to the state capital, Bhubaneswar, where he heard about Congress politicians and ministers consuming alcohol. He returned to Cuttack rather saddened—and wondered if this was what they had all worked for, and passed away the same night uttering 'Oh Lord, show me the light!'

Gopabandhu's wife, Rama Devi, was of a different kind. As a matter of fact, she was not a kind at all; she was a unique person the likes of whom you will not find anywhere. Beautiful, elegant and wealthy, she had deliberately reduced herself to a pauper, with almost no material possessions. Affection, love, and compassion for all beings radiated from her. Her words comforted you in pain, soothed you when you were suffering. An uncompromising idealist, she won you over by her affection, and I never heard her utter a single harsh sentence on any occasion. For the worst offender, she was like a consoling mother. People were in awe of her husband. Everyone loved her. When Indira Gandhi imposed emergency laws upon the country, she went to the city centre in Cuttack, and distributed leaflets urging people to disobey the laws non-violently, and thereby courted arrest at the age of 75. People of Orissa, irrespective of caste and creed, economic status and political opinions, capitalists and communists alike, called her '*Mā*' (mother), and were willing to abide by her mediation when it was called for. She was above politics, and had become all by herself an institution in Cuttack. When Utkal University wanted to confer upon her an honorary doctorate of law, she—who had never gone to school—conceded, for, as she told me, she did not want to disappoint the university officials who were visiting her.

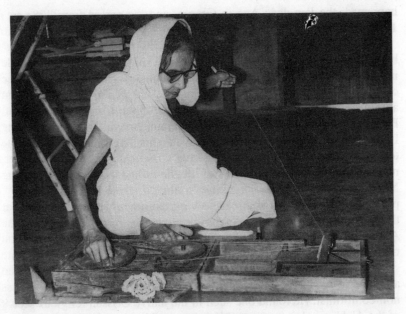

Rama Devi Chowdhury

When the Government of India awarded her a large sum of money for the Seth Jamnalal Bajaj Prize for outstanding social work, she immediately used that money to establish a centre in Cuttack for free early detection of cancer. It is ironic that when she died, Indira Gandhi, then Prime Minister of India, named one of India's coastguard naval ships after her.

Later in life, I had many conversations with Rama Devi. She knew of my early interest in Sri Aurobindo's thought, and recorded in her autobiography, that when she was a young girl, Sri Aurobindo was the first influence on her mind. Gandhi entered her life later. Like Vinoba Bhave, she did not see any incompatibility between their philosophies. As a true Gandhian, she would always wonder, if philosophical thinking could be 'realized' for the good of common people, or for the advancement of social justice. Once she asked me a question that she repeated on several occasions: why is it that at a certain time, i.e., within a certain period, India produced such great minds, and now was barren? She had in mind such giants as Sri Aurobindo, Tagore and Gandhi, Sri Rama-krishna and Vivekananda. In her simple manner, she asked, what did their mothers eat? What penance did they do, to bear such persons in their wombs? I told her of two other periods in world history when this happened: the Periclean Age in Greece, and the period from 1781 to 1832 in Germany.

Nabakrusna Chaudhury, the younger of my mother's two brothers, but older than her by two years, sought with some success, to combine in his life, what I would have liked to combine: an intellectual scepticism, a revolutionary zeal for social justice, and an active political life administering power. A founding member of the Congress Socialist Party, along with Nehru, Jayaprakash Narain, Achyut Patwardhan and Lohia, he later became a Gandhian, gave up his long-time Chief Ministership of Orissa to join Vinoba Bhave's *Bhoodān* (land-gift) movement. But then, in the final years of life, he turned to the ultra-Marxist Naxalites. He was always thinking, trying to arrive at a satisfactory philosophy. In my early youth, he saw me reading a Vedānta work, and thought that old idealistic metaphysics was no good. He found Sri Aurobindo more congenial, since he combined Vedānta with an evolutionary philosophy and promised hope for political action outside and spiritual life within. I think, as he grew older, in one way he was attracted to spiritual ideas, which were non-metaphysical and socially non-conformist. He found one such in the native Orissan religious sect of the *Alekhas*, who were possibly influenced by the Buddhist doctrine of emptiness or *śūnyatā*. He began growing his beard like Ho Chi Minh, and in spite of a stroke he suffered in prison, where Indira Gandhi had put him during the Emergency she had clamped on the country, I found him walking in the summer sun from Bolpur to Santiniketan. In his revolutionary zeal, he became a critic of himself, i.e., of the years he headed the government in the state. I think he was, after his Gandhian years, impatient for social change, and became an ardent supporter of the youthful Naxalites.

As I write this, of the two brothers and their wives, only Malati Chaudhury is alive—somewhat infirm and mentally not quite alert. Last year, during a visit to Orissa, I went to her Ashram in Angul to see her. The Ashram is named after Baji Raut, the young boatman who was slain by the police of the notorious Rājā of Dhenkanal because he refused to tell if the rebels the police were pursuing had crossed the river. This was also the Ashram where Bani and I got married. It was painful to see this woman of undaunted spirit, political and social activist, being pushed in a wheel-chair, and to note that there were no more songs in her voice. When my mother was on her deathbed, in the summer of 1989, Malati sent one of her co-workers with a letter for her. I read out that letter to my mother. Tears rolled down her eyes. They were old friends, and neither wanted to live when the other was gone.

It was among these four people that I grew up, and imbibed Gandhian ideas not as an ideology but as a real force around me. Earlier in my youth, I spun on a spinning wheel—following the Mahatma's example—and used only hand-spun and hand-woven clothes, practiced vegetarianism, walked, if not on bare feet, with a locally made pair of sandals, said, when possible, the evening prayers from all major religions, read and memorized large parts of the *Bhagavadgītā*, washed my own dishes after meals (this was not usually done in middle-class families in India), and tried to cultivate a spirit of empathy with nature and my fellow villagers. It was a way of life—where religion, social activism, and ethical spirit merged together. After finishing high school, I was spending the summer in the village, translating Tagore's poems (originally in Bengali) into Oriya, when I decided to learn tilling the land with a bullock-drawn plough, as was the practice then (and also now). It was hard work, but I wanted to experience what work in the field meant.

My father understood what I was doing, but he was not a Gandhian, and on many matters he held different views from Gandhi and his followers, that is to say, from his in-laws. He would often tell me about what he perceived to be the dangers of Gandhi's non-cooperation movement: when the country became independent, the young people would continue to disobey the law for any and every cause. He was right, as we know today. He did not subscribe to Gandhi's emphasis on using hand-spun and hand-woven clothes. He was amused by my taking to spinning and would have nothing to do with it. In these, and other differences from Gandhi, he was not alone; many of the country's English-educated intelligentsia thought the same way. The poet Tagore, whose admiration for the Mahatma was unbounded, once gave a forceful expression to this line of critique.

My mother did not join her brothers and sisters and their families in their political activities—primarily out of deference to her husband. Since my father was a government 'servant', she did not want to embarrass him by joining anti-government activities. Even my uncles and aunts would maintain a safe distance from him. But I think my mother shared their beliefs and inculcated in us a sense of 'belonging' to the freedom movement. She was a remarkable person—intelligent, strong-willed and principled. She loved her children deeply, but never expressed, nor succumbed to emotions. Devoted to her husband, I never heard the two argue, but as was customary in society then, there was no observable expression of love. I must put on record the deep influence that my mother had on me. She never told me what to do, and had complete faith in whatever I decided to do. The bond between us was never strained by any differences: we supported each other right until the end of her life. When she learned that she had stomach cancer and would not live long, she wanted to be taken to our village home. She did not want to die in a hospital. When I came to the village, she was alert and in peace—although she was in pain. The village doctor, the only one there, was attending to her. Literally hundreds of people—men, women and children—from our village and the neighbouring villages came to see her, to sit beside her and hold her hands. Slowly she faded into a coma, and life slipped away. Something, an invisible tie which connected me to India, to Orissa, to Cuttack and to the village, was severed. I had to be on my own in the wide world. Karl Jaspers wrote to Hannah Arendt on the death of her mother: 'a fundamental change takes place when a person's mother dies ... . The loss of one's mother is the loss of a refuge that has always been there for you, an unconditional affirmation.'

When I left India for the USA, in the January of 1970, I had sent home all my books and papers to my mother. She took care of them in our village home, protecting them from worms and humidity. When she knew she was not going to be around much longer, she wanted me to do something about them. It is not just the library, it is the entire home, a sprawling complex, and the temple of Jagannath which my father built, which need to be taken care of. Real estate in the village is not sold. It is inherited and passed on. Nor are homes rented out. Now things are changing, though. As long as my elder brother is alive, he will look after everything. What will happen after that?

This is how family traditions woven around a village home come to an end. The home in which men and women once lived, where children were born and raised, parties thrown, where there was a continuous hum of activities, visitors, guests, ... will remain vacant, and then, in due course, there will be cracks on the walls, worms will eat away the carved wooden pillars, and it will all be in ruins. All the love and hatred, joys and sorrows, anger and affection which filled it, will become floating memories.

I do not believe in personal immortality, and have found no good reasons to believe in it. Impersonal immortality—meaning that just as my body will merge into the elements, so will my consciousness merge into a cosmic consciousness—makes *sense* to me, but I do not know if it is true. My father and my mother—as far as I am concerned—are irretrievably and without residue gone. So will I. What remains and will remain is memory transmitted through tradition, story, and history. Ancestor worship makes sense—more sense than worshipping an imagined deity.

Calcutta, Oh! Calcutta

Calcutta, the city of palaces, the city of teeming millions, where streetcars ran, and still run, on cobbled streets, where steamers steamed along the muddy Hooghly, where red double-decker buses (which are no more there, alas!) carried loads of passengers along narrow paths—how can one fall in love with such a place? And yet, very soon after arriving, I did fall in love with the city.

Mirzapur Street is a busy street, which meets College Street at one end of the University buildings. I lived in one of the many dark, smoke-filled lanes off Mirzapur Street, sharing a flat with my second brother, who worked as a programme officer at the All India Radio. The stately Asutosh Building of the University stands on College Street where Mirzapur Street crosses it. A little further south stood the Corinthian columns of the Senate House (sadly pulled down now, by unthinking planners and insensitive architects), at the head of whose steps stood a bust of Raja Prasanna Kumar Tagore. The College Square consisted of a square tank around which there was a walk with benches along it. On the side facing the Senate House, there was a statue of Iswara Chandra Vidyasagar, sitting cross-legged on a column (I gather that in the seventies the Naxalites tore down this statue). Further down College Street, separated from the Senate House by Peary Charan Sarkar Street, was Presidency College, which consisted of two huge buildings separated by a green playground: on one side, the main college building, and on the other, the Baker Laboratories. To the south of the Square stood the massive columns of the Sanskrit College, where Vidyasagar was once the Principal. In front of Presidency College, along College Street, and all along the back lanes, there were (and still are) rows and rows of book stores, mostly selling school and college textbooks, and also some invaluable, old and rare books. Hidden among the bookshops, lies 15

College Square, where one stairway leads up to the India Coffee House, and the other to the Aurobindo Pāthamandir (which replaced the old Albert Hall, where the citizens of Calcutta honoured Tagore after he won the Nobel Prize, and where, in response, Tagore opened his heart and gave vent to his anger at the humiliation and unfair criticism that had been showered upon him by the same people who were honouring him only after he was 'recognized' by the West). It is amidst these buildings, and along these streets, that I spent the next four years as a student. For a youth hailing from the sleepy town of Cuttack, it was awe-inspiring. Of the greater part of Calcutta, I discovered very little during these years. Even when I did, it was Calcutta, the seat of culture and politics, which completely captured my interest. The commercial city, the city of wealth (and poverty), of rich businessmen (generally, 'non-Bengalis', a category which was often used, much to my surprise), meant nothing to me. The city I fell in love with was, in my eyes, the city not only of Tagore but of numerous lesser-known poets and writers, the city not only of Aboni Tagore and Jamini Roy, but of many unknown and less-known struggling painters and artists, likewise the city of Pundits and scholars (among whom Raman and Radhakrishnan stood out in their fame), of a great University, (alas! now fallen from its former height), where matters of intellect and heart were widely respected—at least that is how it all seemed to me then.

For the first two years, my life in Calcutta was centred around that stately building on College Street which housed Presidency College. I came to this college with great trepidation. The best students of Bengal—then undivided—used to compete to get into Presidency. Could I compete with them? My credentials from Cuttack meant nothing. I had to begin anew. Climbing up the wide and steep staircase—down which Subhas Bose had pushed a British professor, Mr Oaten, who had used derogatory words about Indians—was breathtaking, literally as well as figuratively. My first philosophy professor was Nalini Kanta Brahma, who had a cold and critical exterior, and wrapped himself clumsily in a wrinkled suit which never quite fitted him. As he walked into class, we were scared. He sat (this, I found out very soon, was his usual practice) quietly for minutes staring at us steadfastly (gathering his thoughts as I surmised later); then he would begin to speak—in measured words, close to the subject matter, never uttering a sentence that was superfluous, going directly to the heart of the matter in the minimum number of sentences. Impressive as a teacher, he soon convinced me that his rough exterior hid a warm heart. He told me he had learned that I was from Orissa, tested me a couple of times (as I discovered later on) regarding my philosophical sagacity, and when satisfied, placed unflinching faith in me. Among my other teachers in the undergraduate class, I must mention Tarapada Mukherjee and Tarak Sen, both of whom taught Shakespeare; Sri Kumar Banerjee (known and often caricatured for his pedantic English), who taught English romantic poetry; but above all, Susobhan Sarkar, who taught European History. I have not, anywhere else in the world, found better, more inspiring teachers.

Among my fellow students in Presidency College—students whose company both provided competition and extended my intellectual horizon—I think of Mohit Sen (later a member of the Politbureau of the Communist Party of India), Shibendu Ghose (who died an untimely death as Indira Gandhi's Defence Secretary), Tapas Majumdar (a famous economist) and Surajit Sinha (anthropologist and later Vice Chancellor of the Visva Bharati).

Life in Eden Hindu Hostel (where I moved from my brother's apartment) was marked by many hours of study, intense political and political-theoretical discussion among peers (most of whom were Marxists of some brand or the other), sipping coffee at the Coffee House at 15 College Square, and joining the proverbial *āddā* of the Bengali youth. Those were the years just preceding India's independence and tragic partition, and in a sense we all were involved, emotionally and intellectually, if not actively, with the freedom movement. Bengal was then ruled by Shahid Sharawardy, leader of the Muslim League. Jinnah's call for the partition of India, and creation of Pakistan was still regarded by us, certainly by me, I recall, as late as early 1946, as a flimsy and not-to-be-taken-seriously idea. Once Jinnah lectured in Calcutta before a large Muslim crowd, and I slipped in to hear him: he was in one of his usual immaculate suits, spoke perfect King's English, had no touch of Islam about him, but appealed to Muslim sentiments against the Hindu majority. The Congress Working Committee was meeting in Calcutta to consider the plan proposed by Sir Stafford Cripps. We went to Ballygunj Circular Road and stood outside the home of Maulana Azad (who was then the Congress President) to watch the members of the Congress Working Committee arrive: Nehru, Kripalani, Pant, and Patel among them. What excitement it was to listen to Nehru later in our college! But all that excitement—largely romantic, patriotic and suffused with faith in humanity—came crashing down when, on 16 August 1946, the great, actually the meanest, 'communal' killings began in Calcutta. Corpses, mostly of Muslims, accumulated in the College Square; Hindus were killed in neighbouring areas. Eden Hindu Hostel, where we lived, was in the middle; on one side was a large Muslim slum (the so-called

Kalābāgān, or 'banana garden'), and on the other side, the Hindu, largely Marwari, locality. The hostel, being a Hindu hostel, as is apparent by its name—a typically British way of keeping the communities apart—was attacked by Muslim *goondās*. We had to accumulate stones on the roof (to be hurled at the advancing crowd), boiling waters to be poured over the attackers, and the walls were covered with live electric wires connected to Baker's Laboratory. Inside, an assistant superintendent of the hostel, who was also an ex-army officer, trained us in self-defence and in keeping a watch from all sides on the attackers. Food was scarce until the Marwari Relief Society brought some in. With the stench from decomposing corpses, one could hardly eat. After two weeks of storm and stress, blood and stinking flesh, when the riot subsided, and the roads opened, some students from Orissa hired a horse-drawn carriage, slammed the doors from the inside, and left for Howrah Station. We squeezed ourselves into a Cuttack-bound train, which was already overflowing with people fleeing the city.

Now Pakistan did not seem merely a frivolous idea of Mr Jinnah. My faith in religion was shattered. How could religion be the reason why innocent men, women and children are killed? (Later, in Germany, a young mathematician, Herr Kleinschmidt, took me by surprise by insisting that nothing was more worthy of fighting for than religion). But my commitment to the Mahatma grew, and I tried to separate in my mind his religious beliefs from the rest of his teaching. As the communal fire spread from Calcutta to Bihar to Delhi and, on the other side, to East Bengal, Gandhi rose to great spiritual heights (naturally, I was trying to identify a sense of 'spiritual', that is independent of a religious point of view). The political leader he had so long been, was changed into a spiritual leader, trying almost single-handedly to restore reason and sanity. When, several months later, I returned to Calcutta, Gandhi was in the city at the height of his greatness, preparing for his visit to East Bengal. My maternal aunt, Malati Chaudhury, accompanied him. Everyone in his entourage risked his or her life, but Gandhi's fearlessness made them go. Stories of inhuman cruelty against Hindus, as well as Gandhi's influence in bringing some sanity back reached us in the city. Some regarded him as an unrealistic dreamer. I thought he was a most realistic worker. From Noakhali, Gandhi went to Bihar, where Muslims were being killed. From Bihar to Delhi, where he met his end. In between, he came to Calcutta to stop the continuing killings, and I managed to slip into the house in Beliaghata, where he fasted nearly unto death, asking both Hindus and Muslims to return their arms. The rest of the story is well known. A few months later, I saw him in

Sraddhananda Park, along with Sarat Basu and Shahid Sharawardy, pleading for the cause of a united Bengal (even if India was to be divided). It all fell on deaf ears. India was divided, so was Bengal. We heard Nehru's speech on the radio. Gandhi fell on the way, he was assassinated on 30 January 1948. As Nehru said, the light had gone out. I was on my way in a train to Ranchi for a vacation when the news reached me. A dark sense of impending doom overtook me.

The final B.A. examination was postponed owing to communal disturbances. Eventually, when we passed the examination, the country was independent. That made me a member of the first group of college graduates in independent India. I stood first in First Class with Honours in Philosophy. Uma Mehta, the second daughter of Gagan Vihari Lal Mehta (later Indian Ambassador to the USA), came second from Scottish Church college. I returned to Calcutta from Orissa in order to enrol for post-graduate classes in Philosophy, and at the same time to join Law College. But where was I to live in the city? The Eden Hindu Hostel was closed to post-graduate students. The college had rented a dilapidated house near the Sealdah Railway Station and converted it into a hostel for post-graduate students. Many of my friends went there. I moved into the Hardinge Hostel of the Law College (where my father had lived many years earlier). Compared to Eden Hindu Hostel, Hardinge Hostel was a beehive of residents, each in a little cubicle. Most 'boarders' were students only on paper: They enrolled at the Law College (the easiest thing to do, as no admission test was required); some enrolled only to get a place to live—they remained students for years (the tuition fee was nominal), while working full time, or being involved full time in student politics. A future Chief Minister of Orissa lived there for years, along with his own cook and servant. For me, the hostel was a blessing. I could study in the University Library (two minutes away) in the morning, then go for philosophy classes during the day, and to Law College in the evening, without stepping outside the campus. Thus, I settled down for years of hard work.

My connection with Presidency College became weaker—even though I was still a student of the college. All our post-graduate classes were held in the Asutosh Buildings of the University. Most of my undergraduate teachers in philosophy had either retired or been transferred to some other place. Nalini Brahma had become the Principal of Hooghly Mohsin College. Jiten Chakrabarty and Baqui Saheb (the two other philosophy teachers) had both retired.

Now in the University's post-graduate department, I met teachers who quietly changed my way of thinking. Nalini Babu had left me with the concern: *Samkara* or Sri Aurobindo? That controversy had been well thrashed out during many meetings at his home. With my friends from and outside the Eden Hindu Hostel, the issue was Gandhi or Marx? We talked endlessly about it, not merely as a theoretical issue but as a living question during the lifetime of Gandhi, and at the height of his greatness. But now theoretical philosophy, in all its ramifications, took hold of me. Three teachers stand out with prominence: Kalidas Bhattacharyya, Rash Vihary Das, and Mahamahopadhyaya Yogendra Nath Tarka Vedanta-tirtha. Kalidas Bhattacharyya was the son of Krishna Chandra Bhattacharyya, who was modern India's most significant and creative academic philosopher (I say 'academic' to exclude such thinkers as Gandhi, Tagore or Sri Aurobindo). When I met Kalidas Bhattacharyya, his father Krishna Chandra Bhattacharyya was still living in his Serampore home, but I never had the opportunity to see him. He passed away when I was still in the post-graduate class. Later on, when I started teaching at the University, Satish Chatterjee, then Head of the Department, and I, worked hard, visiting alumni of the Department all over the city, to collect money for a Krishna Chandra Bhattacharyya Memorial Lecture-ship Fund (to which Humayun Kabir, a former teacher in the Depart-ment, then Education Secretary of the Government of India, gave a matching grant from the Government). Much later, in 1981, the Univer-sity invited me to deliver that lecture. For the present, going back to Kalidas Bhattacharyya, I believe he was certainly the most inspiring teacher I have ever had (possibly with the exception of Josef König in Göttingen). He was not a great orator, and did not use any rhetoric, but he did what very few philosophers do: he thought aloud in class, and by doing so, taught us how to think. He would develop an argument, go through possible objections, to each of which he would develop responses—and in the process he would forget his initial point. There was an utter simplicity about him, both as a person and a thinker, that touched me: no sophistication, no scholarly pretensions, no name-drop-ping but only sheer unadulterated thinking, wherever it might lead. After I passed the M.A. examination, and even after I returned from Germany and started teaching at the University, my discussions with Kalidas Bhattacharyya continued. He left Calcutta University and joined the newly founded Research Department of the Sanskrit College as a Re-search Professor. There, in his office, we—besides me, Pranab Sen, Sibajiban Bhattacharyya, and many others—would drop by to continue our discussions. From outside Calcutta came Daya Krishna, then a young and independent philosopher (he was not attached to any institu-tion). I would go to his house on Janak Road near Ballyganj Lake on

Sunday mornings to talk philosophy, and would stay on until lunch time, when Mrs Bhattacharyya would insist that I join them for lunch. When Kalidas Bhattacharyya moved to Santiniketan, first as Professor, later as Vice-Chancellor—our discussions were interrupted but never quite stopped. Even when I visited India from the USA, I always looked forward to visiting Kalidas Bhattacharyya at Santiniketan. He had then retired, become older—but looked much older than he was because he would not use dentures in place of the teeth he had lost. His whole personality radiated the simple pleasure of thinking. It was contagious. 'I am writing a great deal after retirement', he told me once, and we immediately began philosophizing. My relationship with him—marked by mutual affection and respect—continued. My one regret is that I could not accept his invitation to be a Professor at Santiniketan, but he held no grudge against me for that. In 1981, I was living in Santiniketan with my mother. I was there as a visiting Fellow. He came with his wife to visit my mother, and suddenly, much to my embarrassment, bowed down and touched her feet. When I told him that he should not have done that, he said that it was spontaneous, that he knew who she was: wasn't she the sister of Gopabandhu and Nabakrusna Chaudhury? A year later, I went to Santiniketan to invite him to a small reception that Sankari Banerjee (then Registrar of Calcutta University) and I had arranged in Calcutta, where we planned to present him with a volume of essays we had edited in his honour. Much to my surprise, he said he could not come, for he was afraid we would praise him at such a meeting, and he said it was sinful to listen to one's own praise. I persuaded him to come, assuring him that there would be no words of praise and no lectures except for a few remarks made by me about his philosophy. He agreed, we went to Calcutta together, and took part in a wonderful gathering of many of his students and friends, in the University's stately syndicate room. The news of his passing away came as rude shock, particularly when I learned that his life could have been saved if there had been better medical facilities available in Santiniketan. I lost one whose affection and understanding I had been always sure of. My world became poorer.

Rash Vihary Das was a very different sort of person. If Kalidas Bhattacharyya taught me how to think, and gave me a taste of that pleasure and also the difficulty of pure thinking, Rash Vihary Das impressed upon me the value of rigorous schoarship, combined with the spirit of skeptical questioning. A short and thin person (he thought he was of the same height as Kant), with an imposing beard, he walked briskly with his head slightly bent to the left (he thought, and rightly so, that Kant also walked in that manner—his critics said he had deliberately cultivated such intellectual mannerisms!), always with a book in one hand and an umbrella in the other. He would always smile at one and would tell a joke (which reflected his inner cynicism). Stories abound about his cynicism. I recall only two. In his youth, he lived in Amalner, Maharashtra, at the Indian Institute of Philosophy. The story is that once he went to see the famous Hindu holy man, Lele (who reportedly had initiated Sri Aurobindo into his spiritual life). Lele, learning that his visitor was a philosopher, asked him, 'Why do you dissect God?' Rash Vihary Das replied—I can imagine the ironic smile on his face—'Because he (i.e., God) needs it.' The reply certainly did not please Lele. The other story is based on my own experience. In 1950, just a year after I had passed the M.A. examination, the Indian Philosophical Congress met in Calcutta. Radhakrishnan was the President. I was a volunteer worker, waiting on the dais in the great Senate Hall (sadly, now torn down and replaced by an ugly structure). Rash Vihary Das began to speak on the topic of the discussion in a frail voice: 'Has Sri Aurobindo refuted Samkara's *māyāvāda*?' Radhakrishnan reminded him, 'Rash Vihary, why don't you speak to the microphone? They (meaning the people in the back) cannot hear you.' Quickly came his reply, in the same frail voice, 'But Professor, they won't understand me even if they hear me.' And he continued as before. (Radhakrishnan, on a later occasion when I met him, as the conversation came around to the topic of Rash Vihary Das, said to me, 'Rash Vihary thinks I do not know any philosophy'). Rash Vihary Das, I think, was a complete failure as a classroom teacher. He whiled away his time in class in small talk. But what he was looking for were really able would-be philosophers, and he invited them to his home, where a group of young and not-so-young philosophers met to read books and to discuss problems. (If I remember correctly, he taught Kant's first *Critique* along with Vahinger's commentary to some of us.) In his home, we would meet in his library, which left me with the impression that he had taught himself to read German, French, Italian, Arabic, Persian, and, of course, Sanskrit. He had opened a personal account with the booksellers, Blackwell, in Oxford, through whom he bought books of authors whose names no one had heard of in Calcutta. It is from his library that I borrowed his copy of Husserl's *Logische Untersuchungen* (which he later asked me to keep), in which I developed a life-long interest. His streak of cynicism led him to suspect whether a student who evinced interest in philosophy, and did well in the examinations, was really interested in 'doing' philosophy. He suspected that people who studied philosophy were motivated by some other ulterior purpose. Some, for example, were really interested in religion, and hoped to be able to use philosophy as a means, as a handmaiden, for their religious ends. Others were motivated by political ideologies. For a long time, he suspected that I had some such ulterior motive. He would say, 'Since you are also studying law, you may take to your father's profession; or perhaps you will follow your maternal uncles into politics'. He was often worried when I gave, as I often did, public speeches, for that led him, on one occasion, to remark to me, 'Your real goal must be somewhere else'. He knew of my interest in Sri Aurobindo. One Sunday morning, we were meeting in his house for some philosophical discussion, when Haridas Chaudhuri (who later emigrated to the USA and founded the Institute for Integral Studies in San Francisco, now a University of a sort) sat down beside me and asked me softly how I was. Rash Vihary Das suddenly interrupted: 'Haridas, don't spoil him by your yoga'. (Haridas Chaudhuri was known to be practising Sri Aurobindo's integral yoga.) I eventually learned why he was so suspicious of people who showed an interest in philosophy. During one of our conversations, he told me that for him, as for Krishna Chandra Bhattacharyya, philosophy was 'an autonomous spiritual activity', and should not be used for goals extrinsic to it. In a certain way, this conception of philosophy deeply influenced me. Religion and politics took a back seat.

My interest in Sri Aurobindo, however, continued for some time. I thought I found in him (and later in Krishna Chandra Bhattacharyya) an example of creative thinking which I missed in others in India. As I have said earlier, during my undergraduate years at Presidency College, one of my central philosophical concerns was: 'Are the world and finite individuals real even from the point of view of the highest metaphysical knowledge, as Sri Aurobindo would have it, or is the world, along with finite individuals, only an appearance, *mithyā*, sustained by ignorance (*avidyā*) of the ultimate reality, as Samkara holds?' When in the B.A. First Year class, I published an article entitled 'The Finite and the Infinite' in the Presidency College Magazine, in which I argued against Samkara's *māyāvāda*, and in favour of Sri Aurobindo's conception of integral *brahman*, Nalini Babu, my professor of philosophy (about whom I have written earlier in this chapter), read the essay, and asked me to see him in his house. I went with some trepidation at the appointed time. The house was in a dark smoke-filled lane somewhere around Scottish Church College. The sparse living room with very old furniture and walls showing humidity, and everything almost falling apart, became a place where I visited for the next several months. Dr Brahma, as we called him, wanted to discuss the issues which I found challenging as well as thought-provoking. 'If you did not quite accept Samkara's "non-dualism", that must be because there is some deficiency in my teaching,' he began telling me. Thus began an intensive reading of Sri Aurobindo's texts, interpretation of his arguments against *māyāvāda*, until it seemed as though we were faced with a choice between two alternatives. If Sri Aurobindo was right in his conception of the integral *brahman*, then what he said must be the same as Samkara's thesis. If what he said was different from Samkara's thesis, then he must have been mistaken. How could we decide between these two alternatives? We were stymied. The only way of solving this dilemma, we thought, was to write to the Master himself. So we wrote a letter to Sri Aurobindo, stating very precisely the arguments we had formulated. But how was the letter to reach him? Could we just put it in a mailbox? A bright idea struck me: I knew that the musician Dilip Roy (who lived at the Aurobindo Asrama in Pondicherry) was in the city as a house guest of Raja Dhirendra Narayan Roy of Lalgola. The Raja's son, Biren, was a good friend of mine, and I had been to their house at Merlin Park several times. So I carried the letter to the Raja's house and gave it to Dilip Roy. Dilip Babu was amused and promised to get a reply for us. And very soon he did. Addressed to Dilip Roy, the letter from Sri Aurobindo began with an expression of surprise, that a very distinguished *Advaitin* (meaning Nalini Brahma) had argued that his position was the same as Samkara's. Then he went on to bring out, more perspicuously than anywhere else, what the precise difference was between him and Samkara. As he put it, Samkara's emphasis was on *māyā*, while his emphasis was on *līlā*.

Although Dr Brahma gave me a good grounding in *Advaita*, it was Pandit Yogendranatha Tarka Vedāntatirtha who became my preceptor in Vedanta texts. During one of my usual evening walks around the pond in the College Square, I sat down on a bench beside the great *Pandit*, not knowing who he was. He too was a frequent visitor to the Square in the evenings. Soon we became friends and I gradually discovered who he was—one of the foremost scholars of Mīmāṃsā and Vedānta in the entire country. He told me about his *guru*, Pandit Lakshman Sastri Dravid (whom Sir Asutosh Mukherjee brought from the South to be Professor of Veda in the post-graduate Sanskrit Department of the University), about his many years of teaching at the *Gurukula* near Haridwar (from where many of the now famous *Pandits* of North and Western India studied with him), and then his return to Calcutta. Among his students in Calcutta were Suren Dasgupta, Satkari Mukherjee and Gopinath Bhattacharyya. I joined that distinguished group. (Later, on his death-bed at Chittaranjan Cancer Hospital, he told his son, Sitanshu

Bagchi, that he needed to discharge his obligations to his students. So he dictated to him what he remembered of his students. This collection of recollections appeared under the title *Vidyā Vaṃśa*, i.e., 'The Family of Learning'. His son sent me a copy of this short booklet. One remarkable feature of Yogen Pandit *Mahāśaya* (as we called him) was his astounding memory. I studied with him Samkara's *Bhāṣya* on *Brahmasūtras*, along with the commentary *Bhāmatī* and two sub-commentaries, *Kalpataru* and *Parimal*. I would have the book containing these four commentaries in front of me. He would recite exactly the lines from Samkara and the corresponding lines from the other three texts. (Later, I was to encounter a similar feat of memory in Marburg, where I was participating in a seminar on Kant by Julius Ebbinghaus, son of the famous psychologist, and the last of the great Marburg Neo-Kantians. Ebbinghaus would ask his students to open the *Critique of Pure Reason* at certain pages of the A and B editions (referring to the first and the second editions of Kant's *Critique*), then recite the texts from memory, and go on with his explanations without the book in his hand.) Yogen Pandit Mahasaya knew almost all Sanskrit literature by heart. On Sunday mornings, the living room of his flat on Amherst Street would be full of people—professors, research scholars, and younger students such as me—who would find an opportunity to ask him for references, for texts, or want some explanations of a text, ask him to solve some other scholarly problem (from any branch of Sanskrit learning). He would unhesitatingly, and with enormous compassion, say, '*likhe nāo*' (write it down), and then would recite the appropriate texts, give book and page references, and add his explanations. I know of at least a couple of people who wrote their doctoral dissertations just based on what they learnt at such occasions. The *Pandit* did not worry about what use or misuse people made of his willingness to share his learning. On the contrary, if you did not write down what he said, he would say, '*Aar kothāi pābi nā*' (You will not find this elsewhere). He had no equal. After my M.A. examinations, I was visiting an uncle (who was a member of the Parliament) in Delhi. In his house I met Shyama Prasad Mukherjee (son of Sir Asutosh), then the leader of the Hindu *Mahāsabhā*. He asked me about my studies. On learning that I was studying with the great *Pandit*, he said, 'Learn all that you can from him. There is, and will be, none like him.'

After two years of post-graduate studies, I took the M.A. examinations, which I passed, standing first in the First Class. I had cleared the first two law examinations, but the final examination had yet to be cleared. In the Law College, there were many distinguished teachers—judges and barristers. But one stood out by sheer intellectual power. He was the barrister, Ashok Sen (who would tell us how hard German students worked and how lazy Indian students were!). But now the big question for me was what I was going to do. I had already left the Hardinge Hostel and moved into 80 Park Street, a flat rented by some ex-boarders of Eden Hindu Hostel. The residents—mostly former Presidency College students—were in that in-between, unstable and uncertain phase of their lives, when one has left college but has not found one's 'place' in the world, still not having cut the apron strings of college; when at every available opportunity one visits the college campus (where, except for a few remaining old teachers, no one recognizes you), and sips tea at the college cafeteria, still trying to determine what one should do with one's life. It was during this phase that 80 Park Street offered refuge and hope to us, a group of young men who, it seemed, had no future and were doomed to failure. Of all of us who lived at 80 Park Street, the non-Presidency man, Mani Ghatak, was perhaps the most successful—he was the goal-keeper of the East Bengal, later of the Rajasthan, football team.

I got two part-time jobs teaching 'logic': One at St Paul's College, and the other at the evening section of Surendranath College of Commerce in Ballyganj, across Deshapriya Park. For each job I was paid Rs. 100 per month. I could pay my bills without asking for financial help from my father. But why was I, after all, in Calcutta? Why didn't I just go back to Orissa and seek my fortune there? Two things held me: I was studying Vedānta with Yogen Pandit *Mahāśaya* (and would also discuss philosophy with Kalidas Bhattacharyya whenever there was any available time), and I was falling in love with a girl whom I would eventually marry. A few months later, I think in the autumn of 1950, I got what was then considered a good academic job: a lectureship in the Bengal Education Service, and was asked to join the Hooghly Mohsin College (located in Chinsura, some thirty miles outside of Calcutta). My friends considered me lucky. But if I had to leave Calcutta, why should I not go back to Orissa? With this uncertainty in mind, I was walking along College Street when, at the gate of Presidency College, I met Gopinath Bhattacharyya, who had replaced Nalini Brahma as Professor of Philosophy in the College. He had taught me briefly at the University, and knew me well. The eldest son of the philosopher, Krishna Chandra Bhattacharyya, Gopinath was reputed to be a very careful textual scholar, and a logical and analytical thinker, who was adored by his students.

When I greeted him, he asked me what I was doing. When I told him about the job I had been offered, and my indecisiveness, he asked me if I was in dire need of money. I said, 'No'. He then said, much to my surprise (but, looking back at that moment now, in retrospect, with eternal gratitude), 'Give up the job and study Sanskrit with Ananta *Pandit Mośāya*'. He then and there led me across College Street to the Sanskrit College, past its enormous Corinthian columns, to a huge hall where *Pandits* were seated on raised platforms covered with white linen. He introduced me to one of them and said, 'Pandit *Mośāya*, this is Jiten Mohanty. Please teach him Navya Nyāya. You won't be disappointed.' Thus began years of intense study, which ended only with the great *Pandit's* death in 1967, and was interrupted, with his permission, by the years I studied in Göttingen. If I had not met Gopinath Bhattacharyya on that day, if he had not introduced me to the *Pandit*, and if I had not become his *Schüler*, my life and my philosophy would not have been what they are now. The course of one's life is full of accidents, some of which have far-reaching consequences. Even falling in love is an accident.

There are two kinds of philosophical wisdom: one sees a hidden necessity behind all events, even the most unlikely and improbable; the other sees every event, even the most seemingly planned, to be due to an accidental collocation of circumstances (which might not have been). My inclination was in favour of the latter.

Pandit Ananta Kumar Tarkatirtha was in his fifties—a short, well-built man with large eyes which focused on you as though he was trying to delve deep into your mind. After many years of teaching at Baidyanath Deoghar in Bihar (at the Ashram of Balananda Brahmachari), he returned to the Sanskrit College as Professor of Nyāya and Vedānta. By this time, he had earned a tremendous reputation as a powerful logician with a sharp intellect and a fearless mind. Among his students were: Gopinath Bhattacharyya, Gaurinath Sastri and Pandit Visabandhu Bhattacharya. We developed a close rapport. I had to promise that I would not just stop my lessons midway. He was more than a *pandit* who knew all the texts. He was certainly one of the most intelligent persons I know. He encouraged me to construct new arguments, new *pūrvapakṣa*-s, not to take anything on authority, to try new modes of thinking. At a certain point in my studies, in the mid-sixties, he told me one day, 'Jiten, I am tired of dealing with the same philosophical views—of Mīmāṃsā, Buddhism and Vedānta. I want to respond to new positions. Can you introduce me to some western views?' We tried to read Aristotle's *Metaphysics* and later, Kant's first *Critique*. He was happy and excited. He raised new questions in response to both Aristotle and Kant. As his health declined, he began seeing some holy men. He would come back from his visits disappointed. His mind was too critical to accept anything on faith. He tried to legitimize—on his authority as a *pandit*—some reasonable changes in Hindu ritualistic systems. He even wrote an essay in Bengali, defending the view that all the benefit that accrues from worshipping Durga is mundane and this-worldly: the *pūja* keeps various artisans and specific classes employed, and brings about a social and cultural renewal. His unorthodox views led some *pandits* in Calcutta to write to the government to dismiss him, but he was fearless and stood his ground. I admired him as much for his ability as a logician as for his liberal views on social matters. As I said before, we continued our lessons until his death. He was, during the last months, tired, and had high blood pressure. But nothing gave him more pleasure and boosted his spirits more than intricate issues of Nyāya logic. When he passed away, I took the first opportunity to leave Calcutta for Burdwan. But I will write about that later.

During my students days in Calcutta, I thought as much about Gandhi and his ideas as about religion in the sense of mysticism. After my faith in the established religions was shattered, there still remained the hope that there was the possibility of redemption through cathartic religious or mystic experience. Who could doubt the authenticity of a Sri Ramakrishna, or of a Sri Aurobindo? Nalini Brahma encouraged me to see holy men. He had earlier, during my undergraduate years, directed me to one in Puri. He talked to me about Trailangaswami, and later about Sri Krishna Prem and Anandamayi Ma. I saw Anandamayi Ma from a distance—she seemed to sink into a trance when the devotees sang *mantras*. The beauty and serenity of here face touched me. But what was I to make of it? Nalini Brahma, in his later life (when I lost touch with him) turned to her, and spent most of his time in her *Ashrama*. Krishna Prem and I met during one of his rare visits to the city. His appearance, his voice, and the sincerity of his affection moved me. He asked me about my philosophical interests. He had, he said, left behind his Cambridge philosophical learning for devotion to Kṛṣṇa. It was clear to me that that was not my path. I kept in contact with Sri Dillip Roy—partly due to my connection with Biren Roy's family. Several times, I invited him, and succeeded in bringing him to musical functions at the University. His songs moved me.

I found, among old papers, a letter Dillip Roy wrote to me. I reproduce it below in order to show what I was looking for:

Om

Sri Aurobindo Ashram
Pondicherry

To my friend
 Jittendranath Mohanty

It is love's labour lost to apologize for delay. Love doesn't listen. But the fact is, I have been overwhelmed with work after months of absence. Letters have piled up. I have no secretary. A time was when I had a great enthusiasm for answering questions. Nowadays, I feel I know too little to enlighten others. The only thing I can discuss with some nerve is my Gurudev, and personal experiences and my changed reactions to life. But even these are not easy to express through intellectual language. When I go to Calcutta next (in September) I would like to talk to you in a carefree manner. For I liked your keen enthusiasm and *sraddha*. Nowadays, I have to attend to some dull work for the press. From the morning I had to write letters, one to a Punjabi millionaire, another to a multi-millionaire's daughter. Both of them very fine stuff, and what is more, with some real seeking which their wealth did not answer. But you are fortunate: you are not wealthy, I take it. So I need not write to you. Besides, you know already a great deal and are fairly advanced in philosophy. So my friend, what can I impart to you except my sincere love and felicitations on being philosophic?

Affectionately,
Dilipda

Through Dilip Roy and Nalini Brahma, I came to know Sri Gobinda Gopal Mukhopadhyaya, Sanskrit scholar and singer. This led me to another holy man, Mohanananda Brahmachari, whom, again, I saw from a distance. (Much later, in the USA, I got to know him well, when my daughter, Mitti, took *dikṣā* from him). My relationship with the Aurobindo *Ashrama* continued. (As a matter of fact, as I mentioned earlier, I was introduced to Aurobindo's writings by my high school friend, Aboni Ghosh, who by then was studying Philosophy at Allahabad University. But Aboni's interest in Sri Aurobindo had waned, and he had shaved off his long hair and beard.) I visited Mr Charu Dutta, a retired ICS officer, once a personal friend and then a disciple of Sri Aurobindo. I would go to the Aurobindo Pāthamandir at 15 College Square, next to the India Coffee House, to listen to lectures by visiting scholars and sadhus from the *Ashrama*. Later, after I returned from

Germany and started teaching at the University, I was persuaded by my dear friend Manik Mitra (who then ran the Sri Aurobindo Pāthmandir) to lecture regularly on *Life Divine*. For almost five years, I lectured systematically on that great work from cover to cover—once a month. This gave me an opportunity to study the book in detail and also to get to know a large number of men and women who attended my lectures. After *Life Divine* was finished, I continued lecturing on *The Human Cycle* and *The Ideal of Human Unity*, two other works of Sri Aurobindo. I am told that very few have done what I did over the years, but this also gave me a comprehensive grasp of Sri Aurobindo's thought, although I have been able to write very little on his philosophy. This is one of the things I still hope to be able to do.

I met Dilip Roy again in Europe. While I was in Göttingen, news reached me that Dilip Roy (along with his disciple, Indira Devi, the millionaire's daughter he had mentioned in his letter to me) was in Paris. Jagdish Mehra, a young physics student, and I arranged for his visit to Göttingen, and got the University officials to extend an invitation. Jagdish went to Paris to bring him to Göttingen. When Dilip Roy arrived in town, we found, much to our distress, that the suite at the University Guest House, that we had reserved for him, had been given to Martin Buber, who was to lecture at the University as a distinguished guest. I was delighted to be able to listen to Buber, but complained to the University officials for taking away the suite we had reserved. The University apologized and gave us full use of a castle—actually a castle on top of a hill—the University owned, and placed a car at our disposal for the duration of Dilip Roy's stay. Dilip and Indira were just over-whelmed by the place and the view of the valleys all around. Dilip sang in Bengali, in English, and in German, while Indira danced. Back at the castle, both wrote poems and songs. Indira dictated songs in a trance (as I was told) and Dilip transcribed. That was the last time I saw Dilip Roy. He left Pondicherry, and founded his own *Ashrama* in Poona, where he passed away in the early seventies.

I married the girl I loved. Annada Sankar Roy wrote to me that it was singular good luck. Bani left her home to marry me. My maternal uncle, Nabakrusna Chaudhuri, and aunt Malati gave her in marriage to me in their idyllic *Ashrama* at Angul. Mitti was born a year later. Bani was pregnant with Babuni when I left India for Göttingen. Annada Sankar Roy accompanied me with Punyasloka, his eldest son, to Bombay, to see us off.

After I left, Aboni married Bharati Roy, a close friend of Bani's and mine. They moved to Rajasthan to settle down to a long life of scholarship and teaching. Aboni suddenly passed away in 1992. Bani and I flew from the USA to meet Bharati, alias Mukti-di. Her grief and ours was partly relieved by recalling fond memories of our Calcutta and Cuttack days.

Göttingen: Then (1952–54) and Now (1993)

Then, in the October of 1952, I landed in Genoa—after a twelve-day voyage from Bombay on the ship *Australia*—and took an overnight train to Frankfurt, from where a steam engine brought me, along with three other friends from Calcutta (one of whom, alas! is no more), to Göttingen in the middle of a wintry night. A Catholic mission gave us shelter for the night in their tent, set on the railway platform to receive refugees from East Germany, whose border was close to Göttingen. Very early in the morning, we walked to the university's *Auslandsamt*, or foreign student's office, to announce our arrival. We were sent eventually, after formal preliminaries, to different places—I to the *Studentenheim*, known as *Historisches Colloquium*, at 81 Kreuzbergring, where, with students of history (some of them are now Germany's leading historians), I lived the next two-and-a-half years.

Although I returned to the city several times between 1954–93 for brief visits, it is only now—more than 40 years after I first reached there—that I have returned for a longer stay. In 1952, I came from Calcutta as a young graduate student, coming to the west for the first time, leaving old parents, a young wife and a one-year-old daughter. Excitement about the intellectual world that I thought I was entering was tinged with sadness for leaving a wife, who herself had left her home and family to marry me. That conflict tormented me all through my two-and-a-half year stay—overpowered only by the intensity with which I persisted in learning all that Göttingen had to offer me.

This time I flew on a Lufthansa plane, in the business class, from Philadelphia to Boston, and from Boston to Frankfurt. From the Frankfurt airport I took a train to the city's *Hauptbanhof*, from where an

Göttingen University

ultramodern, superfast, all white and glass streamlined train brought me
to Göttingen. Günther Patzig—a friend from the early fifties, a world-
famous scholar of Aristotle and Frege, now emeritus professor at
Göttingen—was at the railway station (which is all newly built—parts
of which I could recognize as belonging to the station as it was forty
years ago) to meet me. We embraced each other. Patzig used to be a big,
hefty and handsome man, the son of an Admiral in the German Navy in
the Third Reich, blond and energetic, but has now turned into an aging
crouching figure with a beard, who wears blue jeans and a sweater (gone
are his dark grey business suits). We exchanged greetings and marvelled
at how long we had known each other—as did our children. (Mitti got to
know his children when she went from Oxford to spend a few days with
them. We recollected our first meeting in Hamburg (although we had
known of each other, and had even corresponded, having been introduced

by a person we both respected—Rash Vihary Das), and our subsequent friendship during my student days in Göttingen (when he moved to Göttingen as the assistant of Josef König). He drove me through the old town, which, save for a few landmarks, I could hardly recognize. It is all changed, rebuilt, roads redesigned, university building built anew .... I was overwhelmed with sadness. But why did I not anticipate that? We tend to cling to the past. My thoughts drifted to Calcutta, my favourite Indian city, which had not changed that much since I first went there fifty years ago.

The day after I first arrived in Göttingen, on a wintry day in October 1952, I walked to the Kurze Geismar Strasse, a three-storey classical baroque building, in which the Philosophy Seminar was located on the third floor, and the *Kunstgeschichte* Seminar on the second. A beautiful spiral stairway took me upstairs. Outside was written on a tablet—such as may be found all over the town, in memory of its famous inhabitants—that the musician Brahms lived, for some time, in this building (which was two centuries ago a *Frauenklinik*, and that Brahms married the daughter of the doctor in charge of the hospital). As I knocked on the door of the department, a large, handsome, baldish man opened the door, welcomed me in, and introduced himself as Wilfried Stache. Stache was the assistant in the department (in German academia, you are lucky if after your Ph.D. you get an assistantship, thereby providing you the opportunity of writing a second thesis, leading to habilitation, which qualifies you to be a University instructor or *Dozent*). Stache did his Ph.D. with Nicolai Hartmann in Berlin; after the war, when Hartmann became the Professor of Philosophy at Göttingen, he brought in Stache as his assistant. But, to his bad luck, before he habilitated, Hartmann died, and poor Stache was left hanging in the air, with no certainty that he could habilitate (in the absence of a sponsor), and have a career in academia. They were waiting for Hartmann's successor. In the meantime, Hermann Wein—another of Hartmann's *Schülers*—ran the place temporarily. I waited for Wein to come.

Eventually Hermann Wein became my supervisor. A witty, excitable and highly intelligent man, Wein habilitated with Hartmann in Berlin, expected to be an *ordinarius* under Hartmann's patronage but continued to be an 'extraordinary' (ä. o.) Professor after his *guru's* untimely death. Bitter at not being promoted, Wein was happy to have me as his student. Although for my own philosophical thinking, Josef König (who, later, a year after my arrival, came from Hamburg to replace Hartmann) and

Hermann Wein

Helmuth Plessner (the eminent sociologist, Husserl's *Schüler*, Max Scheler's friend) proved more important, Wein was a congenial supervisor to work with, allowing me all the freedom I needed to pursue my own interests and ideas. As a matter of fact, on the eve of my leaving Göttingen after receiving my doctorate, in a farewell party he gave for me, Wein said about me, 'One of my best friends is leaving us. I have only one complaint against Mohanty', he said jokingly but half seriously, 'he has, within these few years, read almost all of German philosophy, but he has not read my books.'

Returning to India, we kept in touch with each other. To every generation of his students—he told me later during a visit—he would mention how hard I had worked. Arriving in Göttingen once, I called Frau König from my hotel. She picked me up and took me to their new house in a Göttingen suburb. Later, perhaps, as far as I can remember, I called Wein from the Konigs' home. He was hurt that I had not got in touch with him first. He said, half in anger, '*Ich dachte, wir sind Freunde*' (I thought that we were friends). He had an anger within him for a world which, he thought, did not treat him well, which did not recognize his talent, so that he never could become an *ordinarius* in Göttingen (only if Hartmann had not died, he would have!). König was always generous with him (as far as I know) but he never could relate to König. I adored König but felt sorry for Wein.

During my student days in Göttingen, I spent more time at the Mathematical Institute and the Max Planck Institute than at the Philosophy seminar. I always loved mathematics. In Presidency College, I wanted to study mathematics along with philosophy, but the college administration did not allow me that combination on 'administrative' grounds. (I was told that not all combinations were allowed, in order to avoid conflicts in preparing timetables.) So I studied Sanskrit instead of mathematics. But I did not learn much of Sanskrit beyond what I had learnt in middle school. When I arrived at Göttingen, my immediate inclination was to enrol myself for mathematics—which I did. Was not Göttingen for centuries the world centre in mathematics—the place where Gauss, Riemann and Hilbert, Klein and Courant, and Weyl and Emmy Nothar taught? I started with a course on calculus with Rallich (who, I heard, was a brilliant mathematician but whose career had come to a halt because the Nazis had favoured him when the greats, Courant and Siegel, left, and Hilbert retired and became mentally incapacitated), then attended the lectures of Lyra (a very sympathetic man, with theosophical and mystical interests) on Number Theory and Analysis, Max Deuring (a brilliant algebraist) on Non-Commutative Algebra, and finally Carl Siegel (at that time, Göttingen's star mathematician, formerly Hilbert's assistant, an *émigré* at Princeton, and just back in Göttingen) on Higher Analysis. I got the taste of pure mathematics, of its beautiful, systematic, often axiomatic elegance, of its freedom from all empirical contents, of the beauty of its deductive demonstrations. I was introduced to the way the domain of numbers is extended from natural to real, from real to complex, and from complex to transcendental numbers. Peanos' axioms impressed me by their simplicity, the Galois groups by their almost magical structure, non-commutative algebras by turning around our naively taken-for-granted ideas of symmetry. Overwhelmed by formal mathematics and its structures, I called upon Carl Friedrich von Weizäcker to seek permission to work in his seminar on the philosophy of mathematical sciences.

Von Weizäcker, whose younger brother, Richard, is—as I write this—the president of Germany, is the son of the Weizäcker, who was Hitler's State Secretary (and was tried in Nurenberg after the war but was set free because he had fallen out of favour with the Führer during the last years, relieved from his position and sent to Rome as Ambassador). He is the nephew of the famous physician and psychologist Viktor von Weizäcker (friend of Freud and founder of the 'psycho-somatic system of medicine') and grandson of the most widely read German translator of the *New Testament*. At the young age of forty, Carl Friedrich von Weizäcker was already a very famous nuclear and astro-physicist; but even twelve years earlier, when president Roosevelt had asked Albert Einstein if the Germans could develop an atom bomb, Einstein wrote to him (much later I saw this letter at the West Point Military Academy) that young von Weizäcker could do it. During the last years of the war, Hitler had put Werner Heisenberg and von Weizäcker in charge of the group that was set up to develop an atom bomb. These two decided to stall the work, so that Hitler would not acquire the bomb—at least that's what I was told by both Heisenberg and Weizäcker. Thus, it is wrong to believe (as many Americans do) that the group *could not* make progress; the truth of the matter is that they *did not* wish to make much progress. At the end of the war, Heisenberg, Weizäcker, Max Born, Otto Hans (all of Göttingen) and other leading German nuclear scientists were taken prisoner by the British and kept under house arrest in England. When I arrived at Göttingen, they had all returned. Otto Hans was the president of the Max Planck Institute (the new name of the old and famous Kaiser Wilhelm Institute of Berlin), Heisenberg, the director of the Max Planck Institute of Physics, and von Weizäcker was Professor of Physics at the Max Planck. Heisenberg and von Weizäcker were close friends. Heisenberg, at twenty-five, persuaded von Weizäcker, then fourteen, to take physics (and then philosophy). Von Weizäcker already had reportedly turned to philosophy, to Plato and Kant and Heidegger. I remember students saying that he was the best-educated man in Germany. Later he told me that he could give up physics but not Greek. He did not actually give up physics, but continued to work on developing the idea of the unity of physics, combining Bohr, Einstein, and Heisenberg, and astrophysics.

I met von Weizäcker in his office one morning and became a member of his seminar for the rest of my stay in Göttingen. It is in this seminar that I came to know Werner Heisenberg, who often joined the class. How exciting it was for me to be in the presence of the discoverer of the Principle of Uncertainty! Once in a party at the *Historisches Collo-quium*, Heisenberg came as a guest, and I danced with his wife.

I became very close with two other Göttingen professors. Both were distinguished German historians: Percy Ernst Schramm and Hermann Heimpel. No two persons could have been more unlike each other. Both were medieval historians. Schramm was perhaps more well known as a historian, one of Europe's most famous medievalists, whose work on the medieval crown and its symbolism led to an invitation—remember, it was just after the war—to become the historical advisor to Queen Elizabeth's coronation! Schramm was a big, open, outgoing fellow. He had been the historian and archivist in Hitler's office during the war, and as a result his lectures in Göttingen on the history of the second world war attracted hundreds of listeners, who spilled over into nearby halls, where loudspeakers had to be installed. Heimpel was reserved, but a kind, very smart, sophisticated intellectual with a unique style of speaking, for which he was adored by his students. He became the rector when I was a student, and continued for many years as the president of the West German Rectors' conference. For some reason, he was enormously kind to me. His wife, to whom I was closer, would often stop by the *Historisches Colloquium*. We would walk together to the grocery and I would accompany her back to her house. The Heimpel family comprised the husband, wife and two children. Their beautiful daughter would often play chamber music with almost professional competence. My life in Göttingen was enriched and beautified by their friendship.

Schramm was known in student circles as having been a Nazi. How otherwise could he have had an office in Hitler's headquarters? But he was smart: after the war, he earned the confidence of the British Army, and played a different role. (According to Günther Patzig's account, during the Nazi era his name was P. Ernst Schramm; after the war he called himself Percy E. Schramm.) He was smart enough to have been able to overcome two serious dangers which normally would have caused his downfall and possibly led to punishment. One was that his niece, Miss Elizabeth von Thadden, a secretary at the headquarters, was involved in organizing the 20 July failed bomb attack on Hitler, and was executed. The other, though comic, could have resulted in serious adverse consequences for Schramm. The then Rector of Göttingen was asked by the Nazi government to send names of the faculty who were opposed to Hitler. The Rector sent a list of twelve names, including Schramm's. General Jodl, the chief of staff, is supposed to have met Schramm with that list. But Schramm was too smart even for Jodl, and found his way out. After the war, the Rector who had sent the names of innocent faculty, explained his action by saying that if he had given only the names of the two who really were anti-Nazi, these two would have been killed, so he added ten more names hoping that not all twelve would be punished! However, the faculty senate retired him early on the grounds that he had lied.

Schramm later visited Calcutta, where I met him again. I never saw the Heimpels again. Heimpel founded and directed the Max Planck Institute for History in Göttingen, and died at a ripe old age. Much later did I learn of the tragedy that overtook him. The family was vacationing in their home in the Black Forest when Mrs Heimpel (to whom, as I have said before, I was closer) was found missing, and was taken to be dead. A month later, she was found *sleeping* (unhurt) deep within the Black Forest. It appeared that she had become confused, and had gone to sleep (with her hairpins neatly laid beside her), and had a heart attack. The children had announced a 50,000 DM reward for anyone who found her. The money went to a mentally retarded young girl, and Elizabeth Heimpel was buried in the Black Forest (Schwarzwald), something she had wanted very much. (Elizabeth was a close friend of Heidegger, and with Heidegger she shared a deep love for the Schwarzwald). Hermann Heimpel, saddened by his wife's death, in his eighties, almost lost his mind, and kept on weeping—not for her but for the fact that when the Jews were being burned he could not do anything. Of every visitor he would ask, 'What should I do now?' (How different he was from Heidegger, who never even regretted his 'political error' but always came up with devious 'ontological' explanations!)

Besides philosophy and mathematics, I also studied Sanskrit, especially Vedic Sanskrit, with Ernst Waldschmidt in the *Indologisches Seminar*. I joined Waldschmidt's class partly out of curiosity to learn how Sanskrit was taught by German professors and studied by German students. (For me, a *Pandit* was the natural teacher of Sanskrit—one who dressed in Indian clothing, was a Brahmin by caste, and taught, squatting on the floor.) In India, during my postgraduate years, I had studied Vedānta with Mahamahopadhyaya Yogendra Nath Tarka Vedantatirtha. I had just begun studying Navya-Nyāya with Pandit Ananta Kumar Tarkatirtha. I have already written about these experiences in the preceding chapter. But I had no experience of studying the Vedas, except trying, in a rather amateurish manner, some *Rig Vedic* hymns, along with a Bengali translation by Matilal Das which I had picked up from a bookstore on College Street. I decided to enrol in the seminar on Vedic hymns that Waldschmidt was offering.

Waldschmidt was of medium height, a stout person with rather black hair—stern in appearance, and as I later realized, also in his relationships. The German students who already knew him were afraid of him in a way and called him *Mahāguru*. His standards were strict and he would not tolerate any deviation. At the time I studied with him, his main research lay in the Tukharisthan Buddhist manuscripts, which he and his graduate students were engaged in editing. He believed, however, that every Indologist should be engaged in Vedic studies at some stage in his or her student life. So this was for him a must, and all his graduate students and assistants were in this seminar—Lienhardt, Schlinglof, Valentina Rosen, Dr Mehendale from Poona, Kusum Mittal from Delhi, a Chinese scholar whose name I have forgotten—altogether twelve of them, including me. (Of those with whom I had become close, and spent hours and hours translating and unraveling Vedic Sanskrit. Lienhardt has just retired as Professor in Stockholm, Schlinglof as Professor in Berlin. Of Dr Mehedale I have not kept track, except that I would often, in India, hear of his reputation. Kusum Mittal once met me in Calcutta, but disappeared from my life after that. About Valentina I will write later.) In that seminar I learned the method of German indologists. Waldschmidt assigned a hymn to each of us. Our task was to translate it into German, point out and resolve problems in translation, identify grammatical problems, and solve them with the help of Pāṇini as well as other Vedic grammars. 'Never use', he warned us, 'any existing translations, never use Sayana's commentary (for, he said, Sayaṇa is closer to us in time than to the Vedic period); use dictionaries, especially *nirukta* and grammar books, and prepare your own translations and report.' And when you presented yours to the class, Waldschmidt would critique you, question you at every step, and tear your arduous work to pieces. He once said to the class, 'My goal is to train you in such a way that given a fragment of a manuscript, you can make something of it, date it, build a reasonable hypothesis about its style, internal and external cross-references, produce a translation, and raise a host of questions.' And in all this, he remained a philologist—an excellent one at that—with no interest in the value and validity of the ideas, concepts, or philosophies of the texts. That is German Indology at its best.

Waldschmidt gave me my final test in the traditional manner of *Salākānyāya*. He put a needle through a palm-leaf manuscript, opened the manuscript where the needle stopped, and asked me to explain just that page—first to translate it, then to point out grammatical problems, and then raise questions and so forth.

I last saw him in Calcutta, where he visited the Sanskrit College, which conferred on him the title of *Vidyārṇava*. We had a nice evening on the verandah of a Park Street apartment where he was staying. He was delighted to see me. After retirement, he donated his house to the Indology seminar. On this visit to Göttingen, I went to that house to give a seminar, and remembered the many occasions when, as a student, I had had dinner with the *mahāguru* and his wife.

Yes, when writing about the Göttingen Indology seminar, I cannot but write about Valentina Rosen. I do not exactly remember where I first met Valentina. It must have been while working in the seminar library, for she had been in Waldschmidt's seminar for a couple of years before me. Before coming to Göttingen, Valentina, the daughter of a German diplomat, had studied in the London School of Oriental Studies, and had done archaeological excavations in Greece. Tall and heavily built, she had a simple and innocent look in her eyes. She was always eager to help, and had a deep and passionate love for India. We became good friends. On Sundays we would often go on long walks to the Nikolausberg. (Surprisingly enough, she never met Wilfred Stache in Göttingen, although Stache lived on the Nikolausberg.) We would often cook Indian food together, along with Kusum Mittal; and then work together on Vedic grammar. After I returned to India, Valentina arrived in Calcutta (on her way to Poona, where she was to do Archaeology), and stayed with us in our Southern Avenue apartment. She and Bani became friends. Mitti and Babuni were small, and Valentina was a strict, though unfailingly affectionate, disciplinarian for our 'uncontrollable' Babuni. It was about this time, somewhat earlier, perhaps, that Wilfred Stache came to India to run one of the Max Müller Bhavans. He and Valentina met, fell in love, and married. They lived for years in Bangalore, in Bombay, in Pakistan—but I never met Valentina again, though I thought of her often. In 1982, I was invited to give a lecture in Göttingen on the occasion of Nikolai Hartmann's birth centenary. There, in front of Hartmann's former residence, where a tablet in his memory was being placed, I saw Stache in the gathering. What a pleasure it was! We embraced, and I asked: 'Where is Valentina?' Wilfred broke down and said, 'She passed away a month ago from stomach cancer.' He had retired from the German diplomatic service, and they had returned to Germany to build a house in a Munich suburb, enjoying a life of retirement—she had all kinds of plans for it—when she fell ill and passed away. We wept together, spent the day walking around the town where we had both lived thirty years ago. About three years later, I got a note from their daughter (who, following her mother, studied Indology in Munich) saying that her father had passed away. I plan to see her, and wonder if she looks like Valentina.

Living in Göttingen, I remember all my old friends. None was closer than Eberhard Bubser, who was a bright, handsome, young freshman at the University. I met him perhaps in the *Mensa*. He had a girlfriend—the two of them were inseparable friends, had been high-school sweethearts, and you never saw one apart from the other. Eberhard radiated an intellectuality that made him stand apart in a crowd. He always had with him his pipe. Having just returned from Oxford, he thought (and said) that there was in Germany no one equal to either Strawson or Austin. He would caricature every professor, and would dismiss every received view with a cynical remark. He became my guide and advisor about everything in Göttingen. He shared with me his candid assessment of each professor. He was good in mathematics but tended to lean towards sociology. Old Kant he understood better than others, for he hailed from Königsberg, where he grew up until the family left by the last boat before the Russians marched in. Without seeing the Baltic sea at Königsberg, he would say, you cannot understand old Kant. Bubser was always short of money. I would have liked him to share my lunch with me, which I would buy. But he was too proud to take any help. During one vacation, I went, along with him and his girl friend, Ina, to their hometown, Lingen, near the Dutch border. I got to know his mother, whom I remember as being a very affectionate person. After I returned to India, Eberhard and I continued to keep in touch. He completed his Ph.D. under Wein, and became Plessner's assistant. I believe, after Plessner's retirement he was left on his own. When I visited Göttingen in the late sixties, I found him living in the basement of a dark, dingy warehouse in the centre of the town. As usual, he had with him his pipe, and he was cheerful but cynical. Ina had left him, and justifiedly so, he said. He earned some money, just enough to keep him going, by translating: I think he translated some of Carnap's writings into English, and some of Strawson's works into German. I told him that, if he wanted to try his luck in the United States, I could perhaps be of help. But he said like Kant in Königsberg, that he would hang around in Göttingen until he found a place there, even if he became old! I believe he knew he was in an abyss. His only inner strength was from his mother. I do not know of anyone who was so close to his mother. I had no news of him for a year after I came to the United States. Then, at last, came a letter from Elisabeth Stroker: Eberhard was dead. The circumstances of his death were most remarkable. He did not have a phone of his own, and would go out to the post office to call his mother (who was sick most of the time). That day, he called his mother from a phone booth. A family friend answered, and told him that his mother had just passed away. Eberhard was found dead in the phone booth with the phone still in his hand. The mother and the son were buried together.

Why is it that this time, in Göttingen, I am thinking so much about two Göttingen women, brilliant and creative, brave and in their own ways

unique, whose lives ended in tragedy? They are Emmy Nothar and Edith
Stein. I have met neither of them. I could not have met either of them. I
heard about both of them when I was a student. But this time I feel close
to them. Nothar lived in Duestere Eichen Weg, close to where I now
live; Edith Stein lived in Untere Carspule 6.

Emmy Nothar is one of the greatest mathematicians of all time, and
single-handedly completed the axiomatic abstract algebra. It was only
after immense struggle, and with Hilbert's support, that she could,
against all odds, habilitate, but had to emigrate to the United States
(being Jewish), where she found a position at the Bryn Mawr College. (I
went to see her grave there on the college campus.) However, her life
was cut short, most unexpectedly, by a surgery that she almost survived.
Among others, Einstein wrote an obituary for her; Hermann Weyl gave
the memorial speech at the college. In Göttingen, she was a legend—even
among the many legends at the mathematics institute. I studied under
one of the so-called 'Nothar Boys', Max Deuring. This time I have been
reading about her 'habilitation' controversy, and the great tragedy of
such a wonderful life and rare talent still haunts me.

Edith Stein was a philosopher. Richard Courant, the mathematician,
brought her cousin (from Breslau) to study with Husserl. Soon she
became a member of the Göttingen Phenomenology Circle, wrote a
dissertation on Empathy—I think under Reinach—and became Husserl's
assistant in Freiburg. She helped put together both the *Ideen II* volume
and the so-called 'Time Lectures' of Husserl. But all her attempts to
habilitate failed, and Husserl's support seems to have been lukewarm.
(Husserl was against 'habilitating' women: in Göttingen he had voted
against Emmy Nothar). Stein seems to have fallen in love with Hans
Lipps (one of Husserl's most brilliant students, who came to philosophy
after being a physician, did a Ph.D. in plant physiology, and habilitated
in the philosophy of mathematics with Courant). Lipps left as a ship's
doctor on a voyage around the world and, coming back, joined the war.
Edith Stein joined a Catholic monastery as a nun—having converted
from Judaism—but was captured by the Nazis in Holland and died in
Auschwitz, eleven months after Lipps fell on the Russian front. I knew
of both—I read about Lipps a great deal, have written about him, and
know that König was a close friend of his. It is now well known that the
Pope initiated the process of 'sanctifying' Edith Stein, and she has been
made a saint. But this time the tragedy, the greatness, the nearness hit me
as a person. I now realize that König was my last link to that circle (as
Deuring was to Emmy Nothar). I wish I had come to Göttingen around
the First World War (but how could I have?). The Göttingen Circle does

not mean much today to philosophers here. Only Patzig knows about it, having been a student of Kurt Stavenhagen. I feel as though I almost 'belonged' to it, as I walk along the streets of this town. I feel 'out of the times'. And I often say to myself, 'They (that is, the people of this town now) do not know the Göttingen I know'. It is an irony that it has fallen to me—an Indian—to keep the thoughts of those phenomenologists alive.

In the summer of 1954, my father died. I knew he was suffering from diabetes and high blood pressure, and was having trouble with his eyes. But he was still on the Bench. The news of his passing away reached me through a family friend, Annada Sankar Roy. The letter from home reached me later. Friends were of great help in my coping with this shock. Father had been always good to me, and had complete trust in whatever I was doing. Emotionally, I was closer to my mother, but my affection for my father was tinged with respect and a certain awe. I knew he felt disappointed when I decided not to finish my law studies in Calcutta, and not become a lawyer (and a judge like him). He had asked me whether I would compete for the Civil Service—knowing fully well that I would not. He wrote to Annada Sankar Roy that he had nothing against my taking up philosophy, but was worried that I would be condemned to poverty. However, he did agree to finance my studies

Girl with the Goose

in Germany, and requested Bani that she ask me—when I was about to leave for Göttingen —if I wanted, after completing my doctorate, to go to London to study for the Bar examination. I had declined. Did I disappoint him in the long run? I hope I did not. When I left Orissa for my trip to Germany, he bade me goodbye in the village where we were staying, and I saw tears in his eyes. Now he was gone. I was concerned about mother, whose attachment to, and dependence on, him was almost total. With him gone, the family finances were in doubtful shape. I could not ask my mother for support. My eldest brother's wife knew very well what my situation was as we were very close to each other. She sold some of her most expensive jewellery, and sent me money. How could I, a poor philosopher, pay her back? She said, 'You don't have to.'

I worked hard to finish my dissertation. Wein, König and Plessner—all three readers accepted it. On a cold winter night, accompanied by friends, led by Frau Fischer (of the *Historisches Colloquium*), I walked to the town centre, climbed up the steps of the fountain, and 'kissed the girl with the goose', which generations of new Ph.Ds over the centuries had kissed. Within a week I boarded a boat en route to Bombay.

I am in Göttingen to write a large book on Husserl. Most of the research has been done in the United States. I receive gifts of prints of articles on Husserl from all over the world in so many languages. My own collection of books on and by Husserl, is more than I would need. There nevertheless were a few items belonging to the late nineteenth-century German philosophy and psychology that I wanted to go through. I attended the lectures of Konrad Cramer (son of the famous philosopher Wolfgang Cramer), who made his theme suit my purposes and devoted it to the relationship of the Marburg Neo-Kantians to Husserl. Cramer and Patzig took part in my fortnightly seminars on Husserl's philosophy of logic. I am amazed at Patzig's sympathetic attitude. He has lost his earlier aggressiveness, although the penchant for making a nice logical point remains. Besides these two, the philosophers at Göttingen have nothing to offer me. What I enjoy is living here, walking on the old streets, identifying old houses, seeing places I knew. Although I had decided not to accept any lecture invitations, some I could not avoid. I attended the Hegel-Kongress at Stuttgart, where I met many interesting Hegel scholars—but did not learn very much. Perhaps one of the more interesting lectures was given by the city's mayor, Oberbürgermeister Rommel (son of the famous General), who could cite Hegel chapter and verse, and also make fun of the philosopher. Then I went to Ram's conference on inter-culturality in Heidelberg. (Here I should introduce Ram Adhar Mall, a former student from Calcutta University, now an *äuberplanmässige* professor at Bremen University. He lives near Köln with his wife Renate and lovely and bright daughter Geeta, who is to be a doctor. Ram has founded and is President of the Society for Intercultural Philosophy, and is also the author of many books and essays on this topic.)

The two universities I had to visit are Köln and Bochum. At Bochum, I spoke on 'Understanding the Other' in Waldenfels's seminar. Waldenfels, whom I have known for the last fifteen years, is a good Husserl scholar, but is now deeply into French phenomenology, especially Merleau-Ponty, Levinas, and Derrida. Since in my lecture I opposed this group of French philosophers, there ensued a highly critical discussion, which went on until noon the next day. Then I left for Köln with my former student Christina Schüs. In Köln, I was invited by Elisabeth Ströker to her seminar. Elisabeth, an old friend, about the same age as I am, is perhaps Germany's best Husserl scholar and has edited several of Husserl's texts. A victim in many ways of German academia's male chauvinism, she has struck back and stood her ground with courage and defiance. We had a lovely evening together; the next morning I spoke to her seminar. I left Köln to spend the weekend with Ram and Renate, who took me to a gathering of Indians in Müllheim near Düsseldorf: for two days Indians belonging to different communities talked about the *Fremdenhass* (xenophobia) which is common in Germany, and discussed the idea of making Germany into a multicultural society. My own views on this matter, at least at this time, is, that unlike America, Germany has an old culture with a history of its own. I would not like to see this culture disrupted by immigrants, who come mostly with economic gain in mind. The immigrant has to learn to appreciate German culture before he can lay claim to the fruits of possible multiculturalism. I know what havoc the idea of multiculturalism (and the accompanying idea of 'political correctness') is causing in America.

In two weeks' time, I flew to England to take the oral examination of a Ph.D. candidate in Oxford; upon my return, Günther Patzig and his wife drove me to the former D.D.R. (East Germany). I went on to Weimar, where Goethe and Schiller lived, to Leipzig, where Bach composed and played, to Halle, where Husserl first taught, and to Jena, where Hegel wrote his *Phenomenology of Spirit*, and finished it on the eve of the Battle of Jena. Then I flew back to the United States.

At the end of these three months, and before I flew back to the USA, I was at a bus-stop, waiting to board a bus on my way to the Philosophy Seminar, when suddenly I saw an older lady. Her face seemed familiar, but I realized that even if I knew her, time and age would have left their mark. Spontaneously I greeted her and asked, 'Did you, in the fifties, live in the *Historisches Colloquium*?' She said, much surprised, 'Yes.' I said, 'So did I', mentioned my name, and asked her, 'Aren't you, or rather, weren't you, Wiebke Fesefeldt?' She hugged me and said, 'Yes, I am now Frau von Thadden.' and she remembered, 'You must be Herr Mohanty.' We both boarded the bus, not even knowing where to begin our conversation, trying to catch up on each other's lives during the past forty years. I was invited for tea the next afternoon to their house. I knew von Thadden as a bright young historian, a former rector at Göttingen. And he had the same youngish, rather boyish face he had then. Wiebke, I recalled, was working with Heimpel, and finished her doctorate, married Rudolph, brought up her four children, and then began writing history books for children. We three tried to recount the story of our lives, and the lives of our children; they told me about other members of the Colloquium. We marvelled at how many of them have become University professors! We talked about German historians. Wiebke thought that even the great ones were 'provincial'. Rudolph differed —certainly Meineke and Schramm were not. However, they still did not do social and cultural history. History for them was political history. Marxism had not touched them (and yet, in a sense, 'history' as a science began in Germany). It is surprising, how many people—professors and students—have told me that it was the student revolution of 1968 which changed everything. Marxism came to stay, while 'revisionist' ones like Habermas lost their appeal. Conservatives became liberals, and liberals became conservatives. The structure and function of German universities were transformed. The old Humboldt vision of University came to be questioned, and is now vehemently rejected by some, and ruefully mourned by others.

From 1968–70, there were, in the United States, the student protests, often violent, against the Vietnam war. Whatever deep scars the Vietnam war left on American life and culture, it did not tumultuously upset the apple cart of the Universities. In Germany, Universities were shaken up and sometimes changed beyond recognition, and yet the 1968 student movement, beginning in Paris, was not against any particular event such as the Vietnam war but against the entire European society and values. Universities in Germany were looked upon as authoritarian—the very few professors (*ordinarius*) were thought to be in their ivory towers ruling their institutes 'from above'. The younger scholars, from the doctoral candidates to the poor *Privat Dozenten*, were at their mercy. The idea of pure science with no social responsibility had held its own. All these were questioned. But with what result?

I remember, Bani and I were in Berlin in 1970 as guests of Berlin Radio, to participate in a several-part radio programme on the response of world religions to the problems facing humankind—problems such as

hunger, over-population and violence. We were invited to a reception by
the President of Frei Universität. He said that his successor was going to
be a graduate student. In the changed constitutions of Universities,
students, staff and faculty had equal representation in the Senate. So in
Berlin, the students and the staff joined together and set up a student
candidate who won. How would he sign his own doctorate diploma, they
all wondered.

Of course, some of those extreme absurdities were corrected, some
changes were rescinded. But the Universities never remained the same.
Now there are few Marxists, still fewer Maoists; as in the United States,
the new generation of students are oriented towards their
careers—the only streak of idealism that remains concerns 'ecology'.
Awareness of the environment and of the 'world' is much stronger in
Germany than in the United States. For me, it has been a great pleasure
that one person, singularly responsible for this awareness, has been
Hans Jonas—a dear friend and colleague from the New School days.
But more about him later.

When I came to Germany as a student, I, of course, did not know about
the concentration camps of Hitler and of the 'final solution' of the
'Jewish Problem'. Most of those I talked to—and not merely students,
but also people who fought in the war—would tell me how little they
knew about it. (I had even heard some people saying that Hitler was all
right except for his policy towards the Jews and his invasion of Russia!)
Those who had a feeling of guilt would say, 'We just did not know what
was happening to the Jews. We saw Jews in our town being taken away
but thought it was for their own security that they were being moved to
safe places. Only at the end of the war did we learn of the terrible things
that happened to them.' This was difficult to believe, but *in some cases*
I have no reason to disbelieve. Patzig told me—and knowing him, I
would believe him—that his father, the Admiral, did not know until
1943 about the mass murders in the camps. Independent of the question
regarding who knew and who did not, I must admit that in India, before
and during the war, there was not only complete ignorance about the
Holocaust but also considerable admiration for Hitler. I remember that
as a high school student, I had read in Indian newspapers—which ones
I cannot now recall—glorious words of praise for Adolf Hitler. These
were not words of praise for National Socialism, or for Hitler's policies,
domestic and foreign. Hitler was praised as a man of great moral and
spiritual power—one who, like the Hindu *brahmacārin*, was a celibate,

a vegetarian, and did not smoke or drink. Besides, he was trying to undo what the British and the French did to Germany at the Treaty of Versailles, and, of course, he was fighting the British, who were India's colonial rulers. I borrowed a copy of *Mein Kampf* from the College Library in Cuttack, and discovered that Indians were not Aryans for Hitler. The true face of Nazism, as well as that of Fascism, was not clearly seen by most Indians (even by some good politicians). Nehru was an exception, and it was he who brought home to Gandhi what Nazism and Fascism meant. Even so astute a politician as Subhash Chandra Bose had hoped that Nazi Germany would help him oust the British from India. The poet Rabindra Nath Tagore had been duped by Mussolini in accepting an invitation to visit Italy as his guest, until Romain Rolland persuaded him to cancel it, after Rolland explained to him what Mussolini stood for.

Even now I have met Indians in the United States, some highly educated scientists and engineers, who (though very rarely) expressed doubt regarding whether the Holocaust ever took place (there are crazy historians everywhere who hold this view) but who (more often) hold the view that the Holocaust is just like many other mass killings that are always taking place around the world. In Germany, or possibly anywhere else, there are people who think that the number of Jews killed is highly exaggerated—that it is not six million, but only two or four million who were killed—as though the seriousness of the crime (and the corresponding intensity of the guilt) depended upon, and increased and decreased with the numbers! They fail to see or confront the almost unique nature and the terrifying face of the Holocaust—the state-sponsored, ideology-driven, bureaucratically organized, cold-blooded attempt to eliminate a whole race without any personal hatred for them.

Since my first visit to Germany, the world and I have learned much more about the Holocaust, and it is very much more on my mind than it was then.

I picked up from a Bochum University bookshop a little paperback booklet called *Heidegger im Kontext*. Heidegger's Nazism is well known, and his *Rektoratsrede* is just disgusting. What this booklet does is to place Heidegger's Nazism in the context of the views, attitudes and decisions of his colleagues in Germany. It contains names of all the philosophers in Germany during the Nazi period, and reproduces data regarding their memberships in the various Nazi Party organizations. The result makes for a most depressing and disgusting reading. Very good philosophers, whom I respected, are shown up as having been members of all kinds of disreputable organizations. (I know that some, like Hans Lipps, became members because otherwise they would not get jobs and would have to starve! But many, I am sure, joined voluntarily; many even joined Chamberlain's despicable research institute on the races!) Josef König, to my utter relief, was completely free from any stain. I knew that König, when he was being considered for the job in Göttingen, was asked to see Bäumler, a prominent Nazi philosopher in Berlin. After a long conversation, Bäumler told him, 'Mr König, you are a born philosopher, and in my view you cannot do anything else. If I take your political views into consideration, you have no chance. But taking into account your special gift, I am going to recommend you.' The famous classicist Karl Reinhart recounts how Lipps got a chair in Frankfurt. When the commission set up to recommend a candidate for the chair of Philosophy in Frankfurt met, two existing *Dozents*, both of whom were Nazis but had no distinguished scholarly record, wanted to be considered. The commission rejected both, and wrote to Heidegger (who was a Nazi) for a recommendation. Heidegger recommended Lipps, who was an excellent philosopher and had just joined a party organization.

When I think of all this, of how German philosophers compromised with the Nazis, my faith in philosophy drops to a low point. I can excuse an ordinary person for not thinking clearly, and for falling prey to powerful propaganda. But philosophers are supposed to be specially adept in thinking. They are supposed to love wisdom. How then could Heidegger, a lover of wisdom, the man who is a self-proclaimed thinker, praise Hitler in his *Rektoratsrede*? In this regard, Husserl and Jaspers stand out as models. Politically conservative though he was, Husserl did not fall into the trap, and as a result suffered indignity because of his Jewish heritage, at the hands of his hand-picked successor.

Why did not Heidegger say even once, after the war, after he had discovered his mistake, that he was sorry? Instead, he indulged in all kinds of obfuscating discourse to confuse and confound. Hannah Arendt told me that Heidegger had told her that he was sorry. But Heidegger never said this in public, in writing! I have been too tolerant of his philosophy. Hannah Arendt taught me to separate Heidegger's philosophy from his political views during the thirties. I have tried to do so, and to be as charitable to his philosophy as I could. But I still have the nagging doubt: is his political mistake totally unconnected with his philosophy?

All these thoughts naturally haunt me while I am in Germany. But something strange happened; I read about it in the German newspapers. On his ninety-eighth birthday, Ernst Jünger—the famed German author, with a shady Fascist past—had two visitors in his home in a Bavarian village—Chancellor Kohl of Germany and President Mitterand of France. How does one make sense of the French President's visit? It is true that Jünger had given up Nazism—to be fair to him, he was never a member of the party—and had even criticized Hitler's policies. Even then the visit was a mystery. My friend, the historian von Thadden, tried to make sense of it but I was not persuaded by his argument.

I returned to Philadelphia on 15 August 1993, after a four-month stay in Germany. Günther Patzig travelled with me, by a glistening Inter-City Express, to Frankfurt to see me off at the airport. Ram and Renate were waiting there, having arrived from Köln. All three were worried about my health and wanted to be by my side when I left. The last week of my stay in Göttingen, I had to be hospitalized for pain in the chest. After numerous and intense investigations, the doctors found nothing. They suspected some sort of coronary problem but they allowed me to leave Germany with the understanding that I would have a thorough check-up in Philadelphia.

A Gandhian Experiment

I returned to India after receiving my doctorate, in the winter of 1954, in a ship belonging to the same Italian company, Lloyd Tristino, whose ship had taken me to Europe. Before returning, I had made trips to England and France—for the first time as a tourist, to see famous places, museums, streets, and shops. I have never been happy playing the role of a tourist. There is something superficial about it—an attitude, or rather a gaze, which objectifies everything, more so with a camera. I have never owned a camera, so I try to remember sights, colours, lights and shades, faces and contours, even the feelings these evoke. In any case, the voyage lasted some twelve days. I read E.M. Foster's *Passage to India*, lying in the cabin, or out on the deck. When that was finished, I turned to Heidegger's *Being and Time*. If there exists an unreal existence anywhere, it is on board a ship.

Disembarking at Cuttack Railway Station, I saw my mother dressed as a widow, and Bani with our two children. Delight and grief were mingled together, as they always are. I went to the village for a few days of rest. Stories of the last days of father were recounted. Mother was reconciled to his death. She had enormous strength within. I saw Babuni for the first time—he was born while I was away. Bani had a difficult time raising the two, especially after father's death. She spent most of the time with my brother and his wife, who took care of the children as their own. I got to know Mitti well and played with her—she would make me crouch like an elephant, and would ride on me; she would sing songs she had learned, and show her tricks. I spent a few weeks with the family, and then I left again.

Vinoba Bhave was entering Orissa at the Midnapore and Balasore border, on 26 January 1955. It had been arranged, through my older uncle Gopabandhu Chaudhury, that I would join his party on that day at that border. It was difficult to be separated again from Bani and the children, and from mother. But Bani agreed that I should not let this opportunity pass. So with a small bag in which I packed the bare necessities, I left.

While at Göttingen I had heard of Vinoba Bhave's *Bhoodān* march, and was eager to get to know him. My uncle had written to me: 'Vinoba has raised the public esteem of philosophy, for he is putting a philosophy into practice'. I had known of him as being, in the Mahatma's own estimation, his foremost disciple. When in 1941, Gandhi started the 'individual *satyāgraha*' movement, he chose Vinoba to be the first to offer *satyāgraha*; Nehru was next. But Vinoba had been a recluse all his life, and a scholar. As the story goes, as a young man he came to Gandhi and sought his permission to live in Gandhi's Ashram in *Sevāgrām*. Gandhi agreed, but he saw no more of the youth. A few years later he again came to Gandhi and sought his permission to take leave to study Sanskrit in Benaras for some years. Gandhi agreed, and soon forgot about him. To the very day, after the promised number of years, Vinoba showed up at Gandhi's. He told me, in the course of a conversation that he would not have left *Sevāgrām* and entered public life if Gandhi were alive. With Gandhi gone, and a communist insurrection in full swing in Telegana, and Nehru preparing to send his army to quell the rebellion and violence, Vinoba decided to act. Nehru agreed to let him make an attempt. Vinoba's *Bhoodān* or land-gift movement started. The story of its beginning is well known and I need not recount it.

The morning after my first conversation with Vinobha, I began walking with him. His daily schedule was as follows: he woke up early in the morning when it was still dark; washed, prayed and gathered his belongings; the party started on its walk an hour before the sunrise; walking along village paths, across rice fields and village greens, across creeks or rivers or whatever is on the way, usually a distance of eight to ten miles to the next larger village. After arriving there, Vinoba took rest; he and the others ate a simple breakfast, which the villagers provided; then, members of the party—or, we *Bhoodān* 'workers' spread out in the village; some collecting statistical data about the village (population, caste breakdown, land holdings, number of landless peasants, other cottage industries, etc.), others going from door to door to spread the message of 'land-gift'; in the evening, Vinoba addressed a public meeting of people from the entire area, sometimes tens of thousands in number; prayer after that; evening meals; *then* the actual 'gifts' would flow in with donors signing over their land-gifts to Vinoba. After Vinoba left the next morning, the local workers would complete the work of 'distribution'. It is thus that 'the god that gives away lands' went walking from village to village. What had I, trained in German philosophy and abstract mathematics, to do with all this?

Vinoba asked me, 'Can you express the philosophy you have learned at Gotrangana (which was his Sanskrit rendering of Göttingen)?' He added, 'The rendering was really Bhandarkar's in your mother tongue, i.e., Oriya?' 'I can try to do it in Sanskrit, to be sure', I replied. He seemed to like that. I asked him what he thought of Sri Aurobindo. His eyes glistened, I knew that because of his Baroda connections, Sri Aurobindo had great influence on Maharashtrian intellectuals. Vinoba replied, 'What can I tell you about Sri Aurobindo? Leaving Gandhiji aside, he has been the most powerful influence on my mind'. 'Let me be more specific,' I said, 'I am very interested in Sri Aurobindo's interpretation of the Vedas. What do you think of it?' This conversation took place as I was trying to catch up with him in the course of our walk together across a rice field in north Balasore in Orissa. As is well known, Sri Aurobindo rejected the alleged 'ritualistic' understanding of the Vedas by Sāyaṇa, and in its place advanced a reading which gave a psychological (or spiritual) interpretation of key Vedic words. (*Agni*, for example, meant, according to Sri Aurobindo, both sensible 'fire' [exoteric meaning] and 'purified will' [esoteric meaning]). I had put this very question to Radhakrishnan, who had reaffirmed the position defended by him in his *Indian Philosophy*—namely the position of Sāyaṇa. Vinoba's response was unique: 'The Vedic texts are capable of a threefold interpretation: an *ādhibhautika* meaning which one finds in the textual records and reflections of the material (social, economic, even political) forces of society *then*; an *ādhidaivika* meaning which one finds in the textual prayers and hymns to gods (á la Sāyaṇa); and an *ādhyātmika* meaning referring to the inner spiritual life of man (á la Sri Aurobindo).' I was impressed by his ingenuity. Later I realized (á la Gadamer) that there is no reason why the possibility of a fresh understanding of a text should be subjected to closure.

After a couple of days of walking, I asked Vinoba if he would teach me some of the Upaniṣads. He agreed, but the only time he could give me was *en route*. So after sunrise, along the way, he would stop, on a field or under a tree, to hold a class for the group, and talk to us about the *Īśa*, *Kena* and the *Kaṭha Upaniṣads*. He attempted to reinterpret Upaniṣadic concepts by discussing their new etymologies (somewhat like Heidegger) in their historical contexts, and also by showing their relevance for contemporary India.

The evening public lectures, always in Hindi, dealt in one sweep with ideas from ancient Indian thought, medieval mysticism, Gandhi, Tagore, modern science and technology, and contemporary political issues. Although he had embarked on the mission of 'land-gift', seldom did he talk about land-gift. I once asked him about this strategy. Vinoba replied, 'My real purpose was spiritual, and not socio-economic'. He also said, on another occasion, 'In ancient India, the philosophers (who were also saints) travelled on foot all over the country, thereby educating not merely the elite but also the common folk. I look upon my *padayātra* or 'journey by foot' as a way, a modern way, of following in their footsteps. I want to educate the common people in matters of ideas—in philosophy'. These lectures of Vinoba during the time I accompanied him bore upon issues from science to self-knowledge, from *vijñāna* to *ātmajñāna*. He emphasized the need for bringing together the two, and insisted that a society founded upon both must be founded upon non-violence. All this was not mere Gandhi. Vinoba did not share Gandhi's anti-science and unhistorical attitude; he sought to bring Gandhi's basic insight into harmony with science and history.

Some time later, after I started teaching in Calcutta, I translated some of Vinoba's lectures in a little volume called *Science and Self-Knowledge*, and also wrote a little pamphlet in my mother-tongue, Oriya, on Vinoba's thoughts, primarily drawing upon my conversations with him.

My contact with Vinoba was lost after he left Orissa. Once when he was passing through Calcutta (I believe he was returning from what was then East Pakistan), I (and my late lamented colleague, Sashi Bhusan Dasgupta) visited him but there was not much occasion for conversation. After I moved to the United States, my mother once visited him at his *Ashram* in Panwar, and I learned that he remembered me and enquired about me.

It was a great disappointment for me when this great man came to Indira Gandhi's defence when Indira imposed her brutal powers upon the country under the pretext of National Emergency. Vinoba defended Indira on the alleged ground that the country needed to go through a period of self-discipline. I am afraid he was not right. Even the wisest of men are sometimes confused in their thinking!

Nabakrusna Chaudhury, Malati Chaudhury, and Rama Devi—all went to prison, this time in independent India. The Mahatma's dream of India was turned into a caricature by someone who shared his surname, and was the daughter of his close political disciple Jawaharlal Nehru.

The Sarvodaya movement, initiated by the Mahatma, has slowly almost died out in my own lifetime, and is almost non-existent today.

Back in Calcutta

I returned to Calcutta at the end of 1955 after an absence of more than three years. I still did not have a job. Bani and the children were left behind in Orissa. The idea was that I should first find a job and a flat, and then bring them over. After brief teaching stints at two local colleges, it did not take me long to be appointed as a lecturer in the graduate college of the University of Calcutta, which was the best I had hoped for. When I look back at how I landed myself in this job, I am convinced that again a curious coincidence of incidents—sometimes misleadingly called destiny—took place. I do not remember why I was on College Street near the University, it must have been sometime in the December of 1955 (a year after I had landed in Bombay). I met Dr Saroj Kumar Das, an old teacher in the University. Saroj Babu, as we called him, had a Ph.D. from London, spoke English with an affected British accent, always wore a finely ironed *dhoti, panjabi* and a shawl with style, had a streak of oratory, did not have the depth of Kalidas Bhattacharyya but impressed his students by a carefully cultivated rhetoric. I was, I knew, one of his favourite students—partly because he was a friend of my younger uncle, Nabakrusna Chaudhury, and his wife Malati, both of whom he had got to know at Santiniketan. Saroj Babu greeted me, asked me what I was doing, and upon learning that I was looking for a job, immediately took me to Haridas Bhattacharya, and introduced me to him in glowing terms. Haridas Babu was a retired Professor of Philosophy from Dacca University, where he had taught at the time the University was at the height of its glory. He had made a name for himself because of his expertise in Comparative Religion, in Psychology of Religion, and also for his oratory. (It is widely known that many philosophers in the past were orators—this phenomenon reached its zenith in Radhakrishnan!) He already knew me; his eldest son, Asoke, and Asoke's wife, Usha, were my friends. He at once took me to the Darbhanga Building of the University; we climbed the majestic stairs, and he ushered me into the office of the Vice-Chancellor. The Vice-Chancellor was a well-known chemist, Sir J.C. Ghosh, who had been Haridas Babu's colleague and friend in Dacca. Haridas Babu introduced me to the Vice-Chancellor as one of Calcutta University's most brilliant students, told him about my doctorate from Göttingen, and said (did not request), 'Jnan, give him a job at this University.' The Vice-Chancellor said, 'I will be happy to have him here but I do not know the situation in the Philosophy Department.' So he sent for Professor Sushil Kumar Maitra, who was the Head of the Department of Philosophy. Sushil Babu came a little later, and when the Vice-Chancellor introduced me to him, and asked if there was a place for me in the department, he said, 'I know Jiten, and if he is appointed, many of my problems will be solved. He can teach many different subjects. But the Vice-Chancellor has to approve a position.' A position was approved and I joined the department soon afterwards. I rented an apartment on Southern Avenue, Bani and the children joined me within a month, and for the first time we lived as a family. The salary was very small; we could just pay the rent and buy groceries. My mother continued to send money for the children for quite some time.

I resumed studies with Pandit Ananta Kumar Tarkatirtha, and a lot of time was spent preparing my University lectures. Professor Maitra was right. I lectured on Indian Philosophy and German Philosophy after Kant; I taught a special class on Ramanuja's commentary on the *Brahmasūtras*, and also a special class on logic. For each of these courses, I tried to make notes, and every year brought the notes up to date. Once I was lecturing on Schelling, and Wilfred Stache was visiting us in Calcutta. I asked him to come to my class and tell me if my lecture on Schelling was up to the mark. He said it was at least as good as that of any German professor he had heard on Schelling. That was very encouraging, for I knew Stache had studied with Nicolai Hartmann (whose book on German Idealism, along with Kröner's *Von Kant bis Hegel*, was the book I was using). For Indian Philosophy, I prepared my lectures only on the basis of Sanskrit texts (some of which I had to read afresh for this purpose), and avoided using English expositions. Several years later, I lectured on theory of knowledge, large parts of which were devoted to theory of meaning and theory of perception. My *Husserl's Theory of Meaning* arose out of these lectures, as did several chapters of *Phenomenology and Ontolgoy*. (Much later, in the early seventies, Hannah Gray, then Dean of Arts and Sciences at Northwestern University, offered me a position at Northwestern, because she was impressed by the fact—as I said in the preface to those two books—that my books arose out of my lectures to students). When Dr Atin Bose—a bright young Marxist—suddenly died, I took over his class on political philosophy, began lecturing on the period from Hegel to Marx, and also offered a special seminar on Hegel's *Philosophy of Right*. I think at that time I was still far from being able to understand Hegel—I had not read his Phenomenology, and was too much under the influence of the neo-Hegelians in my interpretation of Hegel. It was not until the late seventies, at the New School for Social Research in New York, that I began to gain access to the Hegelian mode of thinking, as well as into his texts, especially the *Phenomenology*, which then became one of my favourite texts for teaching. I also taught, in the early sixties, special classes on *Vivaraṇaprameyasaṇgraha* (an Advaita work), and on Samkara's *Bhāṣya* on the *Brahmasūtras*. I recall all this, for looking back I find that the nearest I came to teaching phenomenology was a class on Nicolai Hartmann's *Ethics*. I never lectured on Husserl at Calcutta University, though I used Husserl's *Logical Investigations* (without saying so) in my lectures on theory of knowledge. My Husserl studies were done entirely in the privacy of my home. Navya-Nyāya studies continued at the Sanskrit College. I was not quite sure where all this work was leading me. I was happy and excited but also worried about the direction of my own thinking. I knew that my life was worth nothing if I did not find for myself a 'path of thinking' that was to be uniquely mine.

The Philosophy Department at the University, during my years of teaching, was not terribly exciting any longer. Kalidas Bhattacharyya had left for Santiniketan. Rash Vihary Das had joined the newly founded University of Sagar, although he briefly returned to Calcutta before his retirement. The Head of the Department, when I began teaching at the University—as also when I was a student—was Sushil Maitra, about whom I would like to say a few things. The other senior professor was Dr Satish Chandra Chatterjee, who was well known as the author (along with D.M. Datta of Patna) of a widely used, *Introduction to Indian Philosophy*, and also of a more advanced book, *Nyaya Theory of Knowledge*. After Sushil Babu's retirement, Satish Chatterjee became the Head of the Department, although he never got promoted to become a full professor. The other notable member of the faculty was Dr Adhar Chandra Das: a remarkably intelligent man, he spoke English with the native accent of one from the Sylhet district of Assam, enjoyed finding fault with the English of his colleagues, and taking pride in his own, taught very well, i.e., he always had something substantive to say, had written a book on a negation, and also a critique of Sri Aurobindo—in fact, one of the better members of the group. Of the younger members, Kali Krishna Banerjee (who was still a part-time or rather adjunct faculty) was the one—a few years my senior—I befriended. He was not only very intelligent but he had studied Nyāya with great effort, and was at that time turning towards Wittgenstein and Kierkegaard. With this group, I started and continued as their colleague. With the exception of Kali Krishna Banerjee, all were my former teachers. This shows how inbred Calcutta University was—there were very few faculty members in the University, as a whole, who were not graduates from Calcutta University. In this respect, I prefer the generally accepted American convention that at least in the graduate school you do not hire your own students unless they have already spent years of teaching and research elsewhere. I would like to add that when Sir Asutosh started the graduate college in Calcutta in 1905, he recruited professors from all over India, some very famous names. Now the Universities in India, with the exception of Delhi, are fast becoming provincial, primarily because they are in favour of changing the medium of instruction from English to the provincial language. Even my own appointment to the Calcutta faculty was not entirely uncontested. When the position was advertised, a Bengali professor teaching in Orissa also applied for the same position, and made out his case on the basis that that he was not treated well in Orissa and, therefore, needed to return to Bengal: I, being an Oriya, should go back to Orissa and teach there rather than in Bengal. His argument did not carry weight with the members of the Department, and they hired me despite his objection. It turned out that the Bengali professor in Cuttack owed his problems to the fact that he had two wives, both of whom he kept in the same house.

I have already written about Kalidas Bhattacharyya and Rash Vihary Das. I will now write a few words about Sushil Maitra and Satish Chatterjee, two individuals who loved me and for whom I have admiration and respect, although neither of them meant much to me as far as philosophy was concerned, and neither played any role in my philosophical development. Sushil Babu was unusually tall for a Bengali; he was fair-skinned and had a rather broad forehead with large eyes. He was restless—I never saw him sitting on his chair—and while you talked to him, he would walk up and down or around you, reminding one of Rilke's panther whose 'padded gait ... is like a dance of strength around a centre'. He had red marks on his forehead—signs of his spiritual (we learned, tantric) practices. A very capable scholar in Indian philosophy, also in some areas of western thought, he wrote (and spoke) fluent English and enjoyed criticizing Radhakrishnan (who was the Head of the Department, when Sushil Babu was a young lecturer). Once Radhakrishnan asked him what he thought of him, and Sushil Babu's reply was, 'Professor, you are a first-rate speaker, a second-rate politician, and a third-rate philosopher'. Knowing Sushil Babu well, and the sort of unpleasant truths he could easily pronounce, I can believe that he, in fact, said that to Radhakrishnan. Radhakrishnan, on the other hand, was a kind and generous human being. He always tried to help Sushil Babu and did not let such acidulous remarks dictate his sense of right and wrong. For example, when the Senate of the University was considering a resolution to terminate Sushil Babu's appointment on grounds of unethical conduct, Radhakrishnan came to his rescue, and eloquently praised his scholarship. He pointed out to the Senate that Sushil Babu was irreplaceable. Known to have been a favourite student of the late Sir Brojendra Nath Seal, Sushil Babu was also known to have received from Dr Seal, before the latter's death, most of his unpublished manuscripts. When Sushil Babu was appointed the King George V Professor (later renamed Acharya Brojendra Nath Seal Professor), Shyama Prasad Mukherjee (Sir Asutosh's son) sent for him and reportedly said to him: 'Dr Maitra, I have supported your appointment because I know that Dr Seal's manuscripts are with you, and I hope that after becoming a Professor you will edit and publish them.' Then, after a pause, he is reported to have added, rather ironically but prophetically, 'But I know you will not do it.' Shyama Prasad Mookherjee was right; the manuscripts were eaten by insects in his Serampore house.

Dr Satish Chatterjee's personality was the opposite of Dr Maitra's. A quiet, unassuming and non-aggressive person, he bore his frustration (of never becoming a full professor) silently, always with a smile. I never saw him excited; whether he was angry or he was happy, there would be no change in his demeanour. He always spoke with the same measured way of speaking (you had to wait for the next word, and then for the next sentence). When his wife was dying, he stood by her side, then read some scriptures, and maintained his composure when she died; there was not even a single teardrop in his eyes. After retirement, he sometimes stopped at our house during his morning walks and advised Bani about how to run our household economically. When he was the Head of the Department, and when former students asked him for letters of recommendation, he would ask me (as an Indian teacher he felt he had the right to ask a former student to do this) to write the letter, which he signed and mailed. He instructed me to compose only positive letters—each letter must glorify the student.

Those days, the faculty of the college of Arts and Commerce shared a large Senior Common Room. Only full professors had their own offices. (There was a time when even the professors shared the same Common Room.) There were long mahogany desks with green velvet covers, and we all sat around the desks. There was a partitioned area where you were supposed to talk privately with colleagues or with students. There was a corner where attendants made the tea and toasted the bread. Students came in and went out, looking for their teachers, keeping appointments, discussing studies and examinations—all in the midst of a large crowd of teachers. University politics and faculty 'politicking' were all carried out there in the open. Overlooking this academic market place were photographs of past important academic figures, hanging on the wall in rows. The philosophers, Suren Dasgupta and Krishna Chandra Bhattacharyya, the historian, Hem Roy Chaudhury, the mathematicians, Ganesh Prasad and Pillai, the all-rounder Brojen Seal, were among those figures.

One advantage of the senior 'Common Room' system was that you soon got to know members of all other departments of the college. How else would you get to know Nihar Roy, Suniti Chatterjee, Sukumar Sen, Jiten Banerjee and Anukul Banerjee, Satyen Sen, Pramatha Bisi, Bhabatosh Datta, and many, many others—seniors and famous names who taught in other departments? With some of them my friendship grew. Suniti Chatterjee retired soon after my joining the University but I nevertheless got to know him. Nihar Roy and Satyen Sen became my friends. Satyen Sen, later Vice-Chancellor for a long time, wanted me to succeed him, and as a matter of fact, tried to persuade me to agree (I was then visiting Calcutta from the United States) but I declined. Nihar Roy was one of the few who knew of my intellectual pursuits; he had a European academic background too. When my first manuscript on Husserl was accepted for publication by Nijhoff, I sought his advice about the publisher. He assured me that Nijhoff was one of the world's greatest publishers and encouraged me to sign the contract. Pramatha Bisi, who had great affection for me always would lighten me up with his spontaneous sense of humour. Bhabatosh Datta radiated a natural intelligence and was unfailingly courteous and civilized. There were smarter people in the other departments than among the philosophers.

One person who became a good friend, and whose friendship I thoroughly enjoyed, was the young historian Pradyot Mukherjee. After having spent years in Warsaw, Paris, and London, Pradyot returned to Calcutta as a lecturer in History; but he knew more than history. He had picked up a lot of philosophy and sociology along the way, and we found our interests very finely suited for intellectual conversations. His end came rather soon. When his Polish wife left him, he was shattered. He left for London to try for a reconciliation but in vain, and then went on to Mexico. Somewhere along the way, while boarding a plane, he died from a heart attack. He was a remarkable person. Barun De later informed me that his unpublished papers were at the Social Science Research Centre in Calcutta, and that he had many things to say about me.

My first book in English (I had already published a little booklet on Vinoba Bhave in Oriya)—which was my Göttingen dissertation with a Foreword by Hermann Wein—was put out by the Progressive Publishers of College Street. (The cost was borne by the German Embassy in Delhi: Ambassador Meyer learned about me from Dr Pfauter, then Cultural Attaché and an old Göttingen friend, and offered to help). That book, as I look back at it, was a failure; it made no impact at all—except on a few Hartmann scholars. Most Whitehead scholars overlooked it, for I emphasized Whitehead's Platonism rather than his process-philosophy, which was and still is in vogue. Even after thirty-five years, I find my predilection for Platonism is still strong, and my suspicion of what I have lately called process-dogma, undaunted.

Talking about the Progressive Publishers, I can't but recall, with great fondness, the memory of Sushil Basu, who owned the company, who was a friend of many Calcutta philosophers, and eventually became my friend. A couple of times every week, I would visit his office just opposite the main gate of Calcutta Medical College on College Street. You went through a small clothing store, crossed a courtyard in which people were generally busy lighting coal stoves, climbed up a slippery stairway, and you would see Sushil Babu sitting on his bed. His publishing office, living room, and bedroom were all in one room. You generally expected to find some other University or College professor there, got all kinds of news about the academia, and an unending supply of tea. Philosophy in India will forever be in his debt. He persuaded Gopinath Bhattacharyya to put together his father's works, scattered in various journals, and almost goaded him into writing an introduction to it, resulting in the two-volume edition of Krishna Chandra Bhattacharyya's

Studies in Philosophy. He made me write an introductory essay for an edition of David Hume's *Inquiry Concerning Human Understanding*: that edition is widely used even now, much to my surprise, by college undergraduates. He saw my *Gaṅgeśa's Theory of Truth* through the press, although it is Visva Bharati, and not he, who was the publisher. I could always depend on him for matters relating to publications, and selflessly he laid his expertise at my service. Sushil Babu was a bachelor; and on his passing away, when I was already in the United States, his nephew inherited the company. We all went there for the company of this one man. It is ironic how men and women who contributed towards your becoming what you are leave you alone when their work is done. You go ahead, carrying their memories. You imagine, in fantasy, that they are there watching you.

The fifteen years of my life in Calcutta, 1955–70, were marked by several phases. First, I taught uninterruptedly at the University from 1955–60. From 1960–62, I replaced Kalidas Bhattacharyya, when he left for Santiniketan, as Associate Professor of Indian Philosophy in the Postgraduate and Research Division of the Sanskrit College. In 1962, I returned to the University, but again had to go on a long leave of absence to be the Vivekananda Professor and Head of the Department of Philosophy at the newly founded Burdwan University. However, we continued to live in Calcutta. In 1968, I returned to Calcutta University as the Acharya Brojendra Nath Seal Professor and Head of the Department. In 1970, I left for the United States with a two-year leave of absence and resigned from the chair in 1972—therewith ending a relationship that really began in 1945. I will recount some of the more important and interesting of my experiences during those years.

CHRIS AND JACQUES

In Göttingen, one evening, I was in the *Waschraum*, when I heard a voice in Bengali, 'Jiten-*dā, keman āccho?*' (Jitenda, how are you?). And there was this young man in his twenties, a white-skinned European, with a long dark beard, a sharp nose, a big smile on his face, entering the door. He introduced himself as Jacques Sassoon. He had learned a smattering of Bengali from Amartya Sen and other Bengali friends in Cambridge, from where he had graduated and come to Göttingen to do research in Botany. A grandson of the British poet, Sigfried Sassoon, Jacques was a melancholy person; his sadness grew in Göttingen the more the Germans showed special hospitality to this young Jew coming to Germany soon after the war. As he was walking one evening, with his long beard, a long black coat and a middle-eastern cap on his head, a group of passers-by stopped to look at him, and some among them exclaimed 'Jesus of Nazareth!' Jacques and I became friends (the only other English-speaking student I knew was George Holmes from Oxford, who now holds a chair in History at All Souls College). Jacques had learned to cook Indian food, so we—the four Indian students in the town—would go over to his place to eat Indian curry. About a year after I left Göttingen, as I was sitting in the Senior Common Room in the Asutosh Buildings of the Calcutta University, the same voice sounded again: 'Jiten-*dā, keman āccho*?' There was Jacques again; this time in tattered clothes. He had just arrived in Calcutta, travelling by land all the way from Germany to India. He had given up his scientific research in Göttingen, and wanted to learn Indian music. I took him to our Southern Avenue apartment, where Jacques lived with us for a month or so, after which I found a place for him at 80 Park Street, the same flat to which I had moved from the Hardinge Hostel, nearly six years ago. Jacques stayed there for some time, during which he learned *sitar* from Birendra Kisore Roy Chowdhury (with whom he eventually co-authored a book on Indian music). He then joined the Sangeet Bhavan in Santiniketan, visited the Jewish community in Kerala, and then returned to England. In 1982, I rang him up from Oxford, and we met near Lincoln Inn. He was in charge of the Botany section of the British Museum, still unmarried, still keeping the company of Bengalis (including Amartya Sen, who, in 1982, lived in London and Oxford). We spent hours in a restaurant, reminiscing about how time had dealt with us, for good or for bad.

It was Jacques who one evening brought to our Southern Avenue apartment a friend of his, also from Cambridge, Christen de Linde. Chris, he said, was longing to make Indian friends. He had been in the city for several months as a 'covenanted officer' (as the local euphemism went) with the British merchant firm, Bird & Co. The son of a retired British Army Colonel, Chris went to Harrow, and from there to King's College in Cambridge. Arriving in Calcutta, he discovered that the British merchant companies had strict regulations (or conventions?) regarding which parts of the city they could live in, and the extent and manner of their socializing with the 'natives'. Chris was eager to violate each one of these regulations, and to get to know Bengalis as well as he could. After a couple of visits to our apartment, he asked Bani and me if he could move into our place and live with us as a member of our family. For a number of reasons, this kind of arrangement seemed impossible. To begin with, our apartment was too small. Moreover, in those days we lived as most Bengalis (and Oriyas) did—we ate our meals on the floor of the kitchen; Bani cooked with a portable coal oven, while sitting on the floor. We bathed by pouring water over ourselves with a mug, and so on. But those presumed obstacles (other than the size of our apartment) were precisely the reason why Chris wanted to live with us, rather than with other, more westernized Indians he knew. But what were we to do about the apartment? We rented a small two storeyed house on Raja Basanta Roy Road, in a blind alley. Chris lived on the ground floor, we on the first floor, with the kitchen and dining place on the ground floor. Chris built bookshelves on the walls of his room to accommodate his books; he also set up a wooden platform on which a gas oven could be placed, so that Bani could cook standing up. We decided we would continue to eat on the dining-room floor. Chris insisted that no one should enter the kitchen and dining room with shoes on. And so our joint household was set up. Chris lived with us for six years, and became a part, not only of our small family, but also of the larger family in Orissa. He learned to write and speak Bengali, cultivated the friendship of Bengali intellectuals, and brought all kinds of interesting younger men and women to visit us. He once played the role of *Anthony Phiringi* in a play of that name at the New Empire Theatre. Anthony was an Indo-Portuguese in Calcutta, in the eighteenth century, who became a devotee of *Kālī* and wrote and sang some beautiful devotional songs. For months on end Chris would practise singing Anthony's Bengali songs. At last Chris left the Bird Company, joined the British Council, and after a stint with the Council in Sierra Leone, returned to Calcutta—this time to live at the Theatre Road flat of the Council. His flat on Theatre Road became a place for Bengali intellectuals to visit. There I met Alan Watts, the American hippie poet whom Chris had picked up at the Nimtola Burning Ghat and brought to his flat for a clean-up and some nourishing food. Sometime in the late sixties, Chris left the Council, married Joe (a British woman who came to Darjeeling under the Volunteer Service Scheme and stayed with us for some time in Calcutta), returned to England, completed a master's degree in Linguistics in Edinburgh, taught Linguistics for some time in Hong Kong University, and finally settled down in Paris, running the Institute Brittanique there. Bani and I met Chris and Joe in their Paris flat in 1981. 'How could we not have met for so long?' we wondered aloud. He visited us at All Souls College, where he was my guest for dinner—a ritual which he thoroughly (and, perhaps, perversely) enjoyed, inasmuch as he still took a derisive view of such pretentious exercises.

A NEW UNIVERSITY IN A MAHARAJA'S PALACE

One Sunday afternoon, as I was enjoying one of those siestas which add a special pleasure to the otherwise exhausting Calcutta summers, the doorbell rang. When I opened the door, there stood before me a man, probably in his early sixties, dressed in *dhoti* and *punjabi*, with his hands folded in greeting. I soon learned he was B.K. Guha, a retired ICS officer and the Vice-Chancellor of the newly founded Burdwan University. He asked me point-blank if I would join his University as the Swami Vivekananda Professor and Head of the newly created Philosophy Department. I was only a lecturer at Calcutta University, and had yet to become a Reader. I explained to him that the family could not move to Burdwan, primarily because the children were going to schools in Calcutta (Babuni to St Xavier's and Mitti to Loretto House), and that I did not want to dislocate them or leave the cultural milieu of the city where I had found a niche for myself. He wanted me at any cost, and had no objection to the idea of my commuting from Calcutta. We—Bani and I—thought it over. The financial gain was substantial, and we realized that the move to Burdwan would relieve us form the financial hardships that go with the meagre salary of a lecturer. After a few days of thinking it over, I accepted the offer. Calcutta University gave me a long leave of absence. I persuaded Sibajiban Bhattacharyya, an old friend and one of the leading logicians in India, to join Burdwan as a reader. He agreed, contingent upon the University Library's acquiring a complete set of the *Journal of Symbolic Logic*. I knew I would have no difficulty persuading the administration to buy the compete set. So the Department started with two of us, and two lecturers—Mrinal Bhadra (later to do his Ph.D with me and Kenneth Merrill in Oklahoma) and Sanat Roy Chowdhury (an ex-political revolutionary turned Vedantin, which was not rare in India, and an exceedingly noble and gentle soul).

We started by sitting together in the large library of the former palace of the Maharajah of Burdwan. The palace was a stately pink-coloured baroque building, built in imitation of many such buildings in England. The library was a long hall with bookshelves covering both the long walls. (When I had nothing else to do, I would peep through the dusty glass doors at the books inside, hardly visible. What could a Maharajah's library contain? It contained books on hunting tigers, on jungles, on wars, on the histories and dynasties of kings and queens from all over the world!) I realized why the Maharajah had given away his palace (and adjoining *golāpbāg*, garden of roses) to the University. The upkeep of the buildings must have been terribly expensive, and with the abolition of *zamindari* (the quasi-feudal system of landholding and revenue collection) after Independence, and the Maharajah turning more and more to business investments in Calcutta, it was certainly prudent to donate the dilapidated property for a 'noble' cause! Very soon, the new university buildings were constructed in the so-called *golāpbāg* (which had a wide moat around it, and the garden had hundreds of tall mahogany trees, lined by rose bushes), and the teaching departments moved away from the palace.

I taught at Burdwan for six years—all the while commuting from Calcutta. Commuting on the suburban, newly installed electric trains was an interesting experience. You soon began to make friends. Familiar faces showed up. The vendors who sold their wares—medicines, pens, watches and sundry snacks—got to know you. At the Burdwan railway station, the rickshaw-pullers recognized you as University Professors, and took you to your destination without needing to be asked to do so. Since six hours of my time were spent travelling each day, three days a week, I learned how to make use of the time—reading, marking students' essays, proof-reading, and even doing some writing. A faculty colleague of mine caught me reading *Gādādharī* (supposedly the most abstruse text in the abstruse discipline of Navya-Nyāya), and word went around Burdwan and Calcutta academia to that effect. The three days I commuted, I would come back home so exhausted that I could not study at night. The other days I had to take care of various household chores, attend to the children's studies, and receive friends who dropped by the house in the evening. I could sit down for a stretch of uninterrupted work only after the friends left and everyone else had gone to bed. Thus I developed a habit, which I still maintain, of working late into the night, well past midnight. It was at this time that I was working on my book on Gaṅgeśa's *Tattvacintāmaṇi*, which was published by the Centre of Advanced Study in Philosophy, Visva Bharati in 1966.

SANTINIKETAN

My inner connection with Santiniketan, which I had nurtured in my mind through my aunt, Malati Chaudhury, became institutionalized when Kalidas Bhattacharyya, then head of the Philosophy Department, and later to be the Vice-Chancellor of Visva Bharati, prevailed upon me to join his department as an adjunct Professor. This meant that I would, once a week, after teaching in Burdwan, take an evening train to Santiniketan, rest at night in Ratan-Kuthi, the Guest House, teach two classes the next morning, and take an afternoon train back to Calcutta (and again leave for Burdwan the next morning). The beauty and peace of Santiniketan compensated for the stress and strain involved. The evening I would spend at the Ratan-Kuthi, where I would have numerous visitors—both faculty and students. We would go out to listen to musical performances, stroll along the *sāl-bithi*, stop by Kalidas Bhattacharyya's house for an hour of philosophical conversation. For the first time, I started teaching classes outdoors in the mango groves. In the early morning I would join the morning musical—as was the practice in the *Ashrama*. Exploring the *Ashrama*, learning about the Poet's associations with the buildings, collages, gardens, trees, and paths was enchanting. The Vice-Chancellor at that time was Sudhi Ranjan Das, who was a retired Chief Justice of India. My first morning at Santiniketan, Sudhi-da (as one called him) knocked on my door and offered to take me out for a walk. He said, 'Jiten, I will introduce you to the most interesting things in Santiniketan. They are not the human beings. They are the trees.' He was right. The Ashrama abounds in lovely and sometimes majestic trees—around some of which there have grown legends. Sudhi-da also made me give him my word that Visva Bharati would publish my next book. So I gave *Gangeśa's Theory of Truth* to Visva Bharati.

There were several interesting younger philosophers—younger at that time than I—in Santiniketan, whom Kalidas Bhattacharyya had brought from all over India. They were: Rajendra Pandey, Suresh Chandra, and Dharmendra Kumar from Delhi; A.P. Rao, young Deshpande; G.L. Pandit from Kashmir; Jha from Bihar; and my former students, Reena Mukherjee and Pradyot Mukherjee, from Calcutta. (Many of them are now well known in the Indian academia.) I enjoyed their company. We spent a lot of time discussing our ideas, sometimes what we had written. I also gave them a course of lectures on Husserl's *Logical Investigations*—for the first and the last time, I think, in India. I also got to know the musicians Santi Dev Ghosh, Suchitra Mitra, and Kanika Banerjee. It was easy for me to get to know them, since they all knew and admired my aunt, Malati Chaudhury.

The Santiniketan connection continued until I left Burdwan University in 1967 to return to Calcutta as a Professor. However, I continued to visit the *Ashrama* as long as Kalidas Bhattacharyya lived. Returning to the Ratan-Kuthi aroused nostalgia, but I would go out to look at those magnificent trees. Much later, in 1980 I think, I stayed at the *Ashrama*—in a new Guest House called *Pancavatī*—for three months as a Visiting Fellow. My Presidency College classmate, Surajit Sinha, was the Vice-Chancellor at that time. During those three months—one of the busiest three months I spent in India since moving to the United States—I gave lectures on various topics, in various places: on phenomenology and the social sciences at the China Bhavan, on the structural analysis of a literary work in the Oriya Department, on the Copenhagen Interpretation of Quantum Mechanics at the Physics Institute, on phenomenology and Marxism at Sri Niketan, or Sri Aurobindo at the Sri Aurobindo Centre—not to speak of the various lectures I gave at the Philosophy Institute. I would also commute to Calcutta to give lectures: perhaps the one which drew the most attention was 'Phenomenology, Marxism and Structuralism' at the Institute for Research in Social Science, of which, Barum De, an old friend from the Burdwan days, was the director. I enjoyed life at Santiniketan to the fullest: its music, its beauty and its romantic peace. At the time I was about to leave, I felt one with it, and wondered why I should return to the United States after all. The Poet had been dead for forty years, and I wondered how it was that his spirit pervaded, so subtly, everything around. The Poet not only wrote his masterpieces but transformed the place by adding a new dimension, a new layer of impalpable affective quality to the place. Among those whose company I enjoyed are: the poet Sankha Ghose (who was a Visiting Fellow like me) the cultural anthropologist Baidyanath Saraswati (who uniquely combined a sharp and perceptive intellect with a sensitivity to the Indian tradition), the historian Ashin Dasgupta and his wife, Uma, and, of course, Manasi Dasgupta, at that time the Director of Rabindrasadan.

A few words about Manasi and her husband, the historian Arun Dasgupta. They have been friends of mine since my postgraduate student days in Calcutta, and continue to be friends in whose company I recover continuity with my old self. When I started teaching sometime in the early fifties—I think I was lecturing at St Paul's College and Surendranath College, at both places on a part-time basis—Manasi and Arun lived in an apartment near Kalighat Park. Their apartment became a place for discussion meetings for young college students, and I joined them quite often. Books were discussed, as were ideas. There I met, I think for the first time, Ashin Dasgupta, and also Pratima Bowes, who had just returned from England after receiving a doctorate in philosophy. Ever since then Manasi and Arun have been fostering intellectual *āddā* wherever they have lived—in between they were at Cornell for years, but then again back in Calcutta. Arun Dasgupta also took me to attend the Calcutta Historical Society meetings, and I became a subscriber to the journal *Aitihāsika* (from which I have learned a great deal, especially about Calcutta historians). In those meetings, I first met Ranjit Guha, who is now a distinguished historian and the founder of the school of history known as 'Subaltern History'. Manasi moved from philosophy to psychology (in which she earned a doctorate at Cornell), did academic administration and university teaching, and then returned to do research in philosophy—always full of ideas tempered with a sensitivity for literary and musical creativity. Their son Probal (or Mukur), a fellow student of Babuni, became a dear friend when he was studying linguistics at New York University, and would stop at the New School to discuss his philosophical interests with me.

In 1968, after my return to Calcutta from a semester's visiting Fullbright professorship at the University of Oklahoma, I joined Calcutta University as the Acharya Brojendra Nath Seal Professor of Philosophy. Returning to my alma mater to occupy a distinguished chair was a great pleasure for me. Many of my older friends were still around in the Senior Common Room. But what a change had come about in the course of hardly six years! Suniti Babu had retired, as also Sukumar Sen. Nihar Roy had left for the Indian Institute for Advanced Study as its director. (Each such retirement generated seemingly endless infighting and conspiracies among the intending successors!) The most striking change on the College Street campus was, of course, the disappearance of the stately Senate House, which we had learned to associate with the University; in its place there rose the so-called Centenary Building, which, to my mind, was a poor substitute—as a matter of fact, an ugly structure. In the Philosophy Department, I succeeded Gopinath Bhattacharyya, the eldest son of the world-renowned philosopher, the late Krishna Chandra Bhattacharyya. On joining the department, I discovered that its nature had changed considerably. All my former teachers had retired (thus sparing me the embarrassment of being the only Professor at that time—many of them had been frustrated at not being promoted to the chair); among the new faculty, many were my former pupils, which I thought would make my task of heading the department easier. At least that's what I thought at the time I joined the department. However, I soon discovered that that was not the case, and reality proved to be quite the opposite. The faculty did not quarrel with me, they treated me with deference. But they fought among themselves. There were two warring factions. One consisted of those who championed the cause of Indian philosophy, of teaching Sanskrit texts, and whose interest in and support for western philosophy did not go beyond

F.H. Bradley; the other consisted of all the remaining faculty, who did not like western philosophy any better but still resisted the department's becoming a haven for Sanskrit *pandits*. I had affiliations to both but I saw the future of philosophy in India from a larger perspective than most of them. I was sympathetic to both, though my vision of a philosophical enterprise in the Indian context extended far beyond the narrow parameters of both the warring factions. We struggled hard to change the curriculum (which, as it existed then, was how Sarvapalli Radhakrishnan conceived it to be), and had some success against overwhelming odds. The introduction of more contemporary western philosophy was opposed by the 'traditionalist' camp; and the introduction of more Sanskrit material by the 'modernists'. In concrete terms, it amounted to an opposition of the introduction of subjects that the faculty members did not know. One senior faculty expressed his exasperation once at a faculty meeting in the following words, 'Do you want us to learn these new areas at this age'?

It was during these years that the Naxalite movement began next door—in Presidency College, and College Street was under siege. Mitti was in Presidency, so she knew more about the strategies of the Naxalites than I did. Since the Vice-Chancellor, Satyen Sen, was an old friend, I would spend some time in his office sipping tea (which was brought in continuously). One such afternoon, a dozen Naxalite students came into the Vice-Chancellor's office with (real or imagined) grievances, and would not let us go until they were redressed. We were subjected to what, in the political vocabulary of Bengal then, came to the called *gherāo*, which signified 'being surrounded', and not being permitted to leave unless and until the grievances were redressed, or at least addressed. Satyen Sen would not call in the city's police, to save the University's autonomy. Nor could he, even if he had wanted to, for the telephone lines were cut. A group of fifty students—most of them from Presidency College—shouted slogans, and read out to us, in their more sober moments, from Mao's Red Book; in worse moments, abused and insulted the faculty and the Vice-Chancellor. We were allowed—in their immense mercy—to go to the bathroom but not outside the Vice-Chancellor's office. This went on till the early hours of the morning, when our captors, themselves exhausted, let us go. This was the first taste of an experience which was to be repeated several times during that year. I asked Satyen Sen to relieve me of the Chairmanship of the Department, because in my capacity as the departmental chairman, I belonged to the group against whom political wrath was directed. Amlan Dutta, the Head of the Economics Department, and I shared some of those experiences. (Amlan, known as an anti-Communist, was subjected to much more harassment than I was.) The Vice-Chancellor turned down my request on the ground that I was the only Professor in the Department, and only a full Professor could (now things have changed) be the Head. I was disappointed. I was forty-two years old, and did not look forward to the Headship for another twenty-five years or more. It was at this time that I got a letter from Kenneth Merrill asking to visit the University of Oklahoma. I accepted.

Why did I decide to leave for the United States? There was no good reason for my leaving. I already had a successful academic career. I had become a Professor at the University of Calcutta at the age of thirty-nine—younger than any other occupant of that chair, with the exception of Sarvapalli Radhakrishnan. My research in philosophy was yielding results—both in phenomenology and in *Navya-Nyāya*. There were, of course, irritants: the political extremism on the campus was one such. Another was—which everyone who rents an apartment in Calcutta knows well enough—the landlord of the Fern Road flat, once a close family friend, became a source of harassment. He forced us to move to a flat across the street. The harassment continued on issues not worth mentioning. I did not see an end to this situation while living in the city. Where should I go? Allahabad University offered me their Headship. Delhi was considering an offer. But if I was to be in India, Calcutta was still the place I wanted to be in. Satyen Sen advised me not to resign, and suggested that I take a leave of absence from Calcutta University. I did so, and began preparing to leave for the University of Oklahoma.

Preparing to leave the country was an exhausting matter. Bou (as I called my mother) came to live with us. Chuntia, an old family hand (with whom we all grew up), came to help. Books were packed. Household articles and books were taken by him in a truck to our village home. Those to be shipped to the United States were put into crates and delivered to a shipping agent. I borrowed money from friends to buy four tickets. The little poodle, Alice, had to have a crate to travel in. In the midst of all this confusion, I finished the last committee work I had undertaken at the University: a committee to enquire into malpractices in the M.A. examinations.

An unending stream of colleagues and students came to bid me good-bye. They knew that I was not coming back to the University! The most touching was a visit from Amlan Dutta. Amlan was senior to me in the college by a few years. Known as an impressive speaker, with a clear and analytic mind, a deep humanist and consistently anti-Communist, Amlan had been close to the late M.N. Roy's 'Radical Humanism' group, and later in life moved towards a Gandhian point of view. He became, about the time I was leaving India, a pro-Vice-Chancellor of Calcutta University, later Vice-Chancellor of North Bengal University, and Vice-Chancellor of Visva Bharati. He left his mark everywhere but was harassed by the communists. In any case, Amlan's visit surprised me, for although we knew each other well in the university and on the public forum, we had never met on a personal level. He said that he wanted to make one last effort to dissuade me from emigrating. 'Calcutta University', he said, 'needs you more than the University of Oklahoma does'. I had no reply. I had really nothing to say. I still did not think I was emigrating. There were tears in my eyes. Why then was I leaving? I was not *really* leaving—I told myself (and him). In retrospect, I think, deep within me, I knew that I was emigrating.

Bou went to the airport. Little did she know that I was not coming back to live in India. Or, maybe, she knew. She knew me so well, I did not have to say it.

From the Ganges to the Red River: in Oklahoma in the January of 1970

Afew days before we left India in the January of 1970 for the United States, the apartment was full of crates and packets to be shipped; books and furniture had been sent by a truck to my mother in our village home; friends and students continued to visit us in an unending stream.

The confusion became confounding when the Reserve Bank of India would not let me leave the country (i.e., would not approve my so-called P-form) unless I resigned from my position at the University, on grounds that I was going to the United States with an 'immigration visa' (or, the so-called 'green card'). My argument that the University's Vice-Chancellor had insisted that I go on leave of absence and not resign did not make a dent in the bureaucratic minds of the Calcutta-branch officials of the Bank. So, I wrote a letter to the Governor of the Bank in Bombay (a gentleman who later came to Washington D.C. as India's Ambassador, whom I met at a party in the United States, and he remembered the incident), who immediately, on receipt of my letter, phoned me at the University, and asked me to go to his Calcutta office and collect my P-form. This is a good example of lesser bureaucrats bending a law or a rule to suit themselves, and the effectiveness of directly going to the highest authority. The point of this little episode, however, is that I did not then, not unlike many other immigrants to the United States, perceive myself as an immigrant. I thought, sincerely and honestly, that I would return to Calcutta after a few years teaching and research in the United States—but that was never to be. You become a helpless victim of forces more powerful than your best intentions. In this, no one individual should be singled out as a co-conspirator.

Much later, when I was Head of the Philosophy Department at the New School for Social Research in New York, I wrote to Jürgen Habermas asking whether he would consider joining the New School as Hannah Arendt's successor. 'One does not want to immigrate without reason', he wrote to me, adding that if he were to go anywhere, he would want to come to the New School, provided the circumstances rendered it necessary. What was the reason for my immigration? Did I immigrate 'without reason'? Any reasons that I may give are likely to be afterthoughts, rationalizations after the fact, reconstructions of a narrative. It was another of those historical accidents which have given shape to my life. Hannah Arendt advised me not to judge myself and to let others judge after my life was over—in accord with one of her favourite themes in *The Human Condition*. So began a new phase of my life, a life cut off from my roots. But is not the very idea of 'root' questionable?

OKLAHOMA

Because of my brief visit three years earlier, I was already familiar with the red soil, red rocks, dry grass and bushes, rolling hills and unending plain fields dotted with cattle and the petroleum wells of central Oklahoma. The dust bowl days, when the whole state was covered with dust, and many people emigrated to California in search of a better livelihood, were long over. During the New Deal days, President Roosevelt spent public works money to dig huge lakes and water reservoirs, and, as a result, the state now has a longer coastline of lakes than Minnesota has. And when oil was discovered, the state's wealth increased. Some of this money flowed into the University—but not so much as it did in Texas. The University of Oklahoma was still known for its football team, and not for its academic standing. George Lynn Cross, who was a long-time President, and was the President under whom I joined the University, reportedly said, 'Now we should build a University of which the football team could be proud!' It is to this University that I came—from a great University, the University of Calcutta.

The plane carrying the four of us from San Francisco arrived at the Oklahoma City airport after it was dark, and friends who came to pick us up—Bob Shahan, a future colleague and his wife Lee—drove us to a house which had already been rented for us. Next morning, Bani, Mitti and Babuni had a glimpse of suburban American life as they looked out through the windows. No one was walking on the roads. But for passing cars, there was no sign of life. Coming from the din and bustle of

Calcutta, even at daybreak, they were shocked by the 'lifelessness' of the world around.

But soon they all got busy. Babuni joined Norman High, Mitti enrolled at the University, I started teaching, Bani was initiated by Lee Shahan and other friends—wives of colleagues and neighbours—into the skills and pleasures of grocery shopping, household matters, and American cooking. Life slowly took on a fixed pattern. Calcutta life receded into the distant past, like the receding coastline as your ship leaves a harbour and steams into the ocean.

Whether you like it or not, there is a pre-existent groove, a pre-given pattern, into which your life tends to fall in an American small town like Norman. (Perhaps this is true of life anywhere.) This pattern, which soon holds you hostage in its grip is as much due to the demands, or lack of demands, of American life, as to the fact that you are an immigrant, and there is already an immigrant community (of your ethnic origin) which has predelineated your life for you. The Indian community in Norman consisted then of students, some faculty members and their families, and a few other assorted individuals and families. That was in 1970. Within a few years—certainly by 1980—Indian doctors had moved into the larger Oklahoma City area, and then Gujarati businessmen, motel-owners and grocery shop owners. But let me begin my narrative with what 'Indian Culture' signified or meant to most Indians in a small town like Norman.

First, most Indian families needed babysitters, and Bani being older than other wives (and mothers), and not being in need of money, was politely asked if one could leave a child in the house when needed. (Another reason was, she did not work—most wives did.) Soon, we discovered, there was already a large and complicated network of parties where Indian food was served, songs sung, and what was called 'Indian culture' lived. Once you are in this network, there is no escape. You also throw parties, are invited to more, invite more, and this goes on. You know more and more Indians (here the designation 'Indian' includes, happily for me, people from Pakistan and Bangladesh as well). Easy accessibility to the telephone—in India few of us had phones in our homes, and we certainly did not—leads to gossip, gossip leads to *para-charchā* (discussing others behind their backs), which leads to conflicts and tension. Friendships break (they are, in any case, fragile—forged not out of any inner affinity, commonality of thoughts, but of a common historical destiny of 'being thrown' together as immigrants.) But that does not matter: new ones are forged. A new-comer is pounced upon.

There is something called 'Indian culture' that we all wanted to live and share. This was more due to 'homesickness' and boredom than due to a love for and an understanding of that culture. If I look at it with the eyes of young children who were growing up, in high schools or in colleges, 'Indian culture', for their parents, meant a certain taste in food, music (mostly film songs), *Bhajan* (religious songs), and certain reli-gious rituals. A young person is said to be 'Americanized' if he prefers to eat hamburgers, prefers western music, and does not understand the Bhajan or puja. For many parents, cultivating Indian culture including religious ceremonies, was meant for en-culturing the children, and the latter needed this so that they, when they grew up, do not marry American girls (or boys). 'Understanding' the culture was of no concern to anyone, for no one understood all that, in any case. This perhaps explains why the children in the beginning accompanied their parents to feasts and festivals, but eventually gave up.

Babuni went to Cornell, Mitti to Oxford. With both gone, we were alone. Bani joined the University to continue her postgraduate study in history. The Philosophy Department in Oklahoma was moderately good. It took me a couple of years to pick up a real research programme. I read various things and devoted a lot of my time to the preparation of the graduate courses. My reputation as a Husserl scholar, already estab-lished when I was in Calcutta, got me invitations to conferences and seminars for which I wrote occasional papers, but nothing of great importance came along. One year after my arrival, the University elevated me to one of their distinguished chairs—a George Lynn Cross Research Professorship. I know that some of my colleagues in other departments (not, to be sure, in the Philosophy Department) did not like this, and one of them, a Political Science Professor, actually said to me quite candidly, 'I have been here so long, you just came the other day and got this prized chair.' I said, 'I am sorry, but what could I have done?'

Within the department, relationships were friendly and collegial. Kenneth Merril and his wife, Vanita, have since then remained our best friends in Norman, perhaps in the United States. Carl Berenda, origi-nally Karl Berenda Weinberg, author of a famous book on Mach and Einstein, became a close friend, helped Babuni in his studies in Physics and successfully guided his research for a Westinghouse Prize—but eventually, after his retirement, killed himself out of depression (he had married five times, and his last wife had just left him). Very close personally as well as intellectually to me was also Bill Horosz—Hungarian in origin, a student of Marvin Farber (and earlier at Columbia, of Tillich). The friendship fell apart—much to my sorrow—when Bill Horosz was disappointed with me for not being able to get one of his manuscripts published. (He refused to see me when I visited Norman a couple of years ago.) Bob Shahan, a young, impulsive Northwestern graduate, who chaired the department for a number of years, remained strongly supportive of me until he left academia to work for IBM. The Feavers, Clayton and Margaret continued to be genial friends, as do many others on the campus. The Oklahoma campus failed to inspire me intellectually. It did not provide the challenges that I needed badly at that point in my career. It was a peaceful place to work in provided you do not need external challenges, and know what to do. It was, therefore, at the right moment that I got a telephone call from Aron Gurwitsch from New York to go to New School on a year's visiting appointment. I was thrilled. I accepted the appointment. All this happened during the spring of 1973.

But before I write about New School and New York, I must say a little more about the country that was Oklahoma. For it was here, in the midst of oil wells, prairies and rolling hills that I would spend twelve years of my life. As I write this, I still have a home there—a lovely colonial house made of stone hauled from the Oklahoma hills. Mitti lives there, so in a way that is still the family's home, although I moved to Philadelphia for twelve years. Norman lies almost at the centre of the state. To the north and west of Norman are dry fields where wheat grows in winter, and cattle graze in summer. Around Norman are green rolling hills. To the far east, bordering Arkansas, are mountains belonging to the Ozarks. Oil wells continue to pump black liquid gold all over the state. One can imagine Red Indians galloping across the state—now they are concentrated in certain areas but, unlike many other states, there are no reservations in Oklahoma. Almost every white native Oklahoman has some Indian blood, and people take pride in telling you what fraction that is. The blacks are still poor, and in a city like Oklahoma City, live in ghettos. When I first came to Norman, the town had no black population. Although the sunset law was not in the books, blacks came to work, and returned to Oklahoma City before dusk. Some years later, a black University Professor came to live in Norman, bought a home and settled down. I believe he had to face the wrath of some of the whites. But now things have changed, and I would be surprised if there were racial incidents in Norman. I was always surprised that the native whites clearly differentiated us Indians or 'browns' from the blacks. Indian émigrés all over the United States looked down upon the blacks and thought themselves to be racially, and also culturally superior to them. (I am not sure if they did not also think themselves to be superior to the whites. Even if they did, they did not articulate it; about the blacks, they did not miss any opportunity to do so). This may have something to do with the Indians' negative attitude towards people with black complexion within their own communities, and within India. In many languages, in Bengali, for example, the terms 'fair-skinned' and 'beautiful' are used synonymously. I have always wondered about what could have been the origin of this colour racism. I am told it antedates British Colonial rule, and perhaps goes back to the description of the 'invading Aryans' as 'fair-skinned', and of the native Dravidians as 'dark-skinned'.

Back to Oklahoma. The soil is red. Scratch the green or gray surface a little bit, and you see the red underneath. The river that winds its way outside of Norman—a stretch of sand with a thin streak of water that extends to Oklahoma City—is called the Canadian River. The native Indians believed that the river 'magically' protected Norman from the deadly tornadoes which hit Oklahoma. South of Norman are hills where you can just go and scratch the surface with your hand, and collect 'rose rock' stones—red rocks naturally structured like rose buds. Not long ago, during the 'dust bowl' days, the whole state was covered by dust blown by the wind from the west. The Oklahoma farmers fled to California to start a new life there. This migration has been immortalized by Steinbeck in his novel *The Grapes of Wrath*. In California, they were called 'Okies'. They are still called by that name here in Oklahoma. Some among them are called 'Sooners'; they are the ones who—when the land was opened for settlement—managed to arrive first, illegally, and by jumping the gun, grabbed a lot of land, and continued to bask in that glory and their consequent wealth.

New York City and
the New School

I have spent two stints of teaching at the New School—the first two years as a Visiting Professor, with a leave of absence from Oklahoma, and then, after returning to Oklahoma for a year, three years as a tenured Professor and Chairman of the Department. It was at the New School and in New York that major lines of philosophical research opened up for me and some international reputation came along. What was most important for me was the enjoyment of the friendship of a remarkable generation of (German) scholars. Among them, Aaron Gurwitsch, Hans Jonas, and Hannah Arendt stand out with some pre-eminence in my memory. To this must be added—an opportunity to get to know New York's intellectual life, and to have around me a bunch of highly intelligent and intellectually motivated graduate students.

The move from Norman, Oklahoma, to New York went as smoothly as the move from Calcutta to Norman. New York, in many respects, is like Calcutta—only larger, with taller buildings, and far more dangerous to live in. With all her poverty, Calcutta is a safer place. I could walk anywhere in Calcutta but not in New York, without running the risk of getting mugged or robbed. There is, in both cities, the same intellectuality—without doubt, New York is more intense, more varied, and almost unfathomable. Calcutta has the same love of music as New York. Only Calcutta has nothing like the New York Philharmonic. Calcutta has her poets and writers—like New York. But there is nothing in Calcutta comparable to New York's Harlem, noted for both its crime and its music and dance. There is nothing in New York like Calcutta's College Square with its seemingly endless rows of bookshops and colleges all around it, but where else in the world could there be New

York's Greenwich Village? It is in the Village that I began to work at the New School. Where else other than New York could there be something like the New School? The New School is a typically New York institution, drawing upon talents which only New York could provide.

A word about this unique institution. What is popularly and affectionately known to New Yorkers as the New School, is the large adult-education division of the School located on 12th Street at Sixth Avenue, which offers non-credit courses in any conceivable subject—from pornography to Yoga, from Chinese poetry to African dance, taught by experts in these fields, by men and women who have established themselves in life but want to teach just for the sake of teaching. There could be Walter Cronkite teaching journalism, or Paul Newman teaching movie-acting. The New School became a forum where, as John Dewey, one of its founders, said, you can teach (and learn) subjects not falling within the boundaries of traditional academia. I had nothing to do with this division of the School. The division where I taught is the Graduate Faculty of Social and Political Science, located on the east side of Fifth Avenue, between 14th and 13th Streets. The 'Graduate Faculty' has a romantic history that needs to be sketched for those who do not know about it.

Alvin Johnson, President of the New School at that time, decided to approach the Rockefellers for help in setting up an academic institution for social scientists who, under the threat of Nazism, were fleeing Europe. He reportedly left 12th Street en route to the Rockefeller Plaza, with the thought of asking for ten thousand dollars, but as he walked those forty-six blocks, his estimate and request grew 46 times ($10,000 for each block, as he recounted). With support from benefactors, the New School established its graduate faculty as the home for a group of brilliant emigrees, mostly German social scientists. This group included the political economists Staudinger and Adolph Lowe, the Gestalt psychologist Max Wertheimer, the sociologist Alfred Schutz, philosophers Hans Jonas, Aron Gurwitsch and Fritz Kaufmann, and later, Hannah Arendt. It became 'the little Heidelberg on the 12th Street'. In a reception at the home of the Dean, I heard Frau Staudinger remark, 'When my husband became the Dean, he first hired American Caucasians to the faculty'. Hiring me, an Indian, certainly required still greater willingness to change. Gurwitsch was to retire in a couple of years. He wanted me to succeed him but I had to try it out myself as a visitor.

A medium-built, short but handsome man, Aron Gurwitsch was a Lithuanian German Jew, genial and courtly, single-mindedly committed to his work without letting himself be distracted by other contending and conflicting philosophical ideas. Gurwitsch's original training, in Göttingen, was in mathematics and gestalt psychology; later he went to Freiburg to attend Husserl's lectures and drew the Master's appreciative attention. His wife, Alice (alias Raja), was, in her youth, a spirited woman from the German city of Fulda (where I used to visit during my student days in Göttingen), a gifted painter, an active Zionist, always by Aron's side in his work. The extent to which Aron's mind was exclusively focused is shown by the following stories. When he was a refugee in Paris, he dined regularly with a man whose company he enjoyed. Years later he learned that he was the Russian mystic-philosopher Gurdjiff. Gurwitsch told me he never had any philosophical conversations with him. After coming to the United States, when he earned his living by teaching mathematics and physics at Harvard, he got to know the logician Quine. His friendship with Quine continued but they never discussed their respective philosophies (Quine's could not be more different from Gurwitsch's). I always felt that Gurwitsch thought and wrote as though he was still in the same academic world which he was forced to leave. As soon as the war was over, and Nazism was eradicated, he returned every summer to Germany! He still thought of himself as a German, and also as a Zionist Jew. During my first lecture at the New School, Alice Gurwitsch sat in the front row, and after I finished, she came up to me, congratulated me and said, 'You lecture like Aron, you have the same clarity and analytic skill.' Two years later, when Gurwitsch suddenly passed away while vacationing in Zurich as a guest of the Plessners (I will write about the Plessners later in this story), I succeeded him to the chair to which he had almost nominated me.

After Aron's death, my friendship with Alice continued. She would send me, every Christmas, a wonderfully hand-painted or etched card—which adorn my bookshelves to this day. Once when Bani and I were visiting her, she asked me if I wanted to take any of Aron's books from his library. I preferred to ask her for Aron's Göttingen 'hood' (he had a Ph.D. from Göttingen), which I now use for ceremonial commencement processions. The papers went to Yale's Beinecke Library.

Gurwitsch did not fundamentally affect or influence my philosophical research. I was already working on lines which were close to his, so he just found my work congenial. But two colleagues at the New School, in many ways introduced me to new ways of thinking, and thereby slowly and imperceptibly, affected my rendering of 'phenomenology'. They were Hans Jonas and Hannah Arendt. Jonas and Arendt were very different kind of thinkers from Gurwitsch. Gurwitsch was a Husserlian in the strict sense. He thought with almost mathematical rigour and clarity. Jonas and Arendt were closer to Heidegger, though by no means Heideggerians, and thought, with a profound concern, about the historical destiny of human existence. Gurwitsch thought ahistorically. All three were Zionists, but Arendt, by the time I arrived, had, owing to her unorthodox reporting on the Eichmann trial in Israel, fallen into disfavour with the Jewish community—so much so that her two colleagues misunderstood her, and even stopped speaking to her. And yet Jonas and Arendt were friends from their youthful Marburg days.

Jonas, in his youth, had made a mark for his work on the history of Gnosticism, which made him the leading scholar in the world in that field. He wrote a ground-breaking book, *Phenomenon of Life*, in which he followed a Whiteheadian line—arguing against the Husserlian primacy of subjectivity. In the early seventies, he was into the philosophy of technology and medicine. He was the first philosopher who had been asked by the US Congress to testify regarding the value of genetic technology. At the time I got to know him, he was writing his work, later to have a great influence in Germany, on modern technology and ethics. In the late eighties, he became almost a guru for the German youth. Germany named one of their Intercity trains after him (and another one after Arendt). The last time I met him—he visited us in our Norman home—he told me that none of his books had such sales as his book on technology and ethics in the German version. I asked him how he was enjoying his retirement. He said, 'Mohanty, when I was teaching at the New School, I had three days off. Now, after retirement, I have none.' As Europe recognized, adored, and rewarded him, he worked harder. I got his postcard from Madras, 'I should have talked to you before I came out to India. These temples have overwhelmed me'. He passed away on his flight back from Rome, where Italy had just honoured him with one of the country's most distinguished prizes.

To write about Hannah Arendt is difficult for me. Her very being was so completely intellectualized, so wholly given to ideas, that I could not imagine her to be personally close to anyone. Yet she drew me to her with a deep personal affection. During the few years that I got to know her, there grew such a relationship between us that it now seems to me as if I had known her all my philosophical career. Her pictures from her early life and from her Marburg and Freiburg years, show her to have been extremely beautiful. Her youthful face carried the stamp of her deeply thoughtful nature. By the early seventies, when I met her, the experiences of pain and suffering under the Nazis in Germany, and later in France, and the disappointments in her personal life had left their mark on her face. But her overall intellectuality would nevertheless light it up, concealing that pervasive sadness. Heidegger, with whom she had an affair in her youth, had disappointed her; Karl Jaspers, her eventual mentor and lifelong correspondent, was gone. Her first marriage to Alfred Stern, Husserl's student, had broken up, though the marriage with Hans Blücher in New York proved to be solid and based on profound mutual respect. Success came slowly in the United States, but when it did come, she received her due. (The *New York Times* obituary on her death described her as among the ten most influential intellectuals in the world, and certainly the most significant woman philosopher.) She rejected Heidegger's offer to renew their old relationship, yet she was capable of deep friendship: Karl Jaspers, Hans Blücher and the New York authoress, Mary McCarthy, were amongst her closest friends.

A person of strong views about others, she once told me she found that the Dean at the New School had lied to her; she never spoke to him after that discovery. I think she regarded all Straussians as dishonest because Leo Strauss had not been honest with her (they were colleagues in Chicago). As I noted earlier, she was a Zionist, and while in New York, had helped European Jews to emigrate to Israel. But when she disapproved of Israel's policies, she never hesitated to speak out, despite consequences that were not pleasant for her personally. Intellectually, she was not willing to make compromises. Notwithstanding Heidegger's Nazism and personal betrayal, she never let those experiences influence her judgment of the Master *as a thinker*. I felt—and her posthumously published Gifford lectures confirmed—that she had a category called 'thinker', which was so elevated above the life of action, *vita activa*, that very few qualified for inclusion. This small group included Socrates, Kant, Husserl, Wittgenstein, and Heidegger. She herself was one of them. Ideas, pure ideas, moved her.

'Why did you want to hire me for the New School, when there were many others, including German and French scholars, in the field of Phenomenology?', I once asked her. 'You are not only the best,' she replied, 'you also know the classics [she thought of Sanskrit]. Most present-day philosophers do not.' I learned later on, to what extent she went to make it possible for me to move to New York. The following is an instance. Learning that my wife was not willing to come to New York, she started calling her trying to persuade her, making her promise not to let me know that she had been talking to her. It came as a surprise to me when Bani changed her views about the move and began insisting that we accept the New School offer!

I was the chairman of the department when Hannah Arendt died. She was talking to a French reporter in her study, full of books, when she suffered a heart attack and fell on the floor. I buried her—near her husband, who had predeceased her—on the campus of Bird College on the Hudson, north of the city.

There was no longer a compelling reason for me to continue to live in New York, and I began thinking about moving out.

But what I had learned and imbibed at the New School has sustained me to this day. Gurwitsch confirmed or validated my understanding of Husserl and my work on him. From Jonas, I learned that the existential significance of philosophy need not be understood in narrowly pragmatic terms. Arendt gave me a sense of both the historicity of ideas and their eventual ahistoricity. From all of them, I derived a renewal of the importance of *thinking* for my own existence. All three had become urban intellectuals—they pined for New York's intellectual and artistic society. I loved New York but never came into its grip. The rustic villager in me lived on and I did not mind going back to Norman, for I knew what I had to write.

The only unpleasant experience at the New School came almost at the end. When I resigned my position, Albert Hofstadter, whom I had persuaded to come from California, became hostile towards me, which came to me as a surprise. Hofstadter was a New Yorker, who taught very successfully for many years at Columbia, and then moved to Santa Cruz, California. His earlier work on analytic philosophy and aesthetics was overshadowed by the reputation he had acquired for his marvellous translations of Heidegger's works. We invited him, along with Anthony Quinton of Oxford (now a Lord), to replace Jonas and Arendt. A highly cultivated person, sophisticated in the New York style, Hofstadter related very well to me. He threw a party to which Bani and I were invited. When he learned that I had resigned, he thought I had let him down, and even suggested that I might not enjoy the party. I told him that I would go, and I did (without Bani). I enjoyed the party—his wife would not talk to me but Al was pleasant (outwardly). But his meanness, which caught me off guard, knew no bounds. He even warned the Dean that I might move some of Husserl's papers (from the Husserl Archive) to my own library. The Dean saw the absurdity of his suspicions and asked me not to be bothered about it. Once, much later, when I was at the New School for a Ph.D. defence, I extended my hand to him but he did not take it, claiming that it was too early for reconciliation. Years later, I saw him in Berkeley—he congratulated me on the success of my Husserl and Frege book, and thought we could be friends again. I always wondered how a marvellously civilized person could demonstrate such anger for no apparent reason, and for an imagined cause—namely, that

I had conspired to bring him to New York (from his Santa Cruz ivory tower), and then let him down by leaving the New School!

Sometimes philosophers can show a face that does not serve the cause of their noble profession well. As chairman of the New School, I took enormous pains to get the school's Board to approve of my efforts to invite Jacques Derrida—at that time, he was not a household name among intellectuals—to join the faculty. When I was negotiating his salary with the Dean, I received a letter from Derrida cancelling the negotiations, informing me that he had decided not to come to the New School because the letter of appointment that I had sent him earlier did not specify the salary he was going to receive. This was frustrating and annoying—I had told him that the salary offer would come from the Dean.

After I left the school to return to Norman, Oklahoma, Quinton also returned to Oxford as the Master of Trinity, after which he became the President of the British Libraries and a member of the House of Lords. When I visited All Souls College in Oxford, we—the Quintons, Bani, and I—spent some lovely hours together. When I was trying to hire Quinton at the New School, I asked Isaiah Berlin if he would write a letter about him. Berlin wrote, among other things, that Quinton was possibly one of the most well-read British philosophers since David Hume. That was high praise, true, if of anyone, of Isiah Berlin himself. But there was no doubt about Quinton's erudition. Jonas was sceptical regarding my decision to hire him, and he told me so. But, in a few days, Jonas met Quinton at a dinner in his house. They talked for hours, and the next day Jonas told me, 'Mohanty, you made the right decision.' Quinton could talk on any subject, read many languages, was an effective teacher, and above all, he was a friendly person and a generous colleague. New York life suited him well. His wife Mircea's family owned one of New York's famous department stores and a home in Southampton on Long Island. Quinton enjoyed a good life, good clothing, and a feast of ideas. I found his sense of humour and witty style refreshing. With his great wit, he constructed a definite description which he claimed holds good of me and of no one else: 'The one and only x who is a specialist in Navya Nyāya, Husserl, and Frege'.

The glorious days at the New School ended in the summer of 1978. We returned to Norman and bought a beautiful colonial house with a stone exterior, a wood-panelled interior, and redwood ceilings. Life took a turn towards peace and quiet, and I started writing down all the thoughts that New York had stirred within me.

Oxford and Freiburg

I

In 1982, I was elected a Visiting Fellow of All Souls College in Oxford University. Matilal, an old friend from my Sanskrit College days who had studied logic with me before going to Harvard for graduate work, saw to it that I spent some time at All Souls. All Souls, a stately and beautifully chiselled college on High Street, is perhaps the only college in the world which has no students. It consists of Fellows—internal and external. Radhakrishnan had been a Fellow for many years. So were many distinguished British academics as well as politicians. The Fellows administer the college and its vast landed property and real estate in London. The Professorial Fellows draw their salary from the University and lecture. The other Fellows are maintained by the college; they do their own research or teach undergraduates of other colleges (in Oxford 'teaching' means 'conducting tutorials for undergraduates'), for which they receive some extra money. The college provides rooms or apartments and free meals. Since at the time the college was founded the Fellows were churchmen, it is no wonder that only male fellows were admitted and no fellows could live, within the college premises, with families. When I was there, the first woman was admitted. For families (and so for me and Bani) the college provided an apartment in the village of Ifley on the Thames. I could take free lunch and dinner at the college, but Bani could not. There is a ladies' day each term, when ladies can be invited by the fellows for dinner but a fellow could not bring his own wife as a guest. So, you have someone else invite your wife, and you invite his. These are the remnants of social conventions of centuries past. But the college, and the University, stick to them as far as possible.

By contrast, academic life in the United States has very few conventions. There is no dress code—either for faculty or for students. At All Souls, I had (most reluctantly) to live by the rules. For example, a bow tie and gown were required for dinner (but not for lunch, which was happily informal). Even more exacting is the conversation you are expected to carry on at the dinner table—you do not talk about weather, about politics, or about academic themes. What else is left? After dinner you go for wine and cheese to another room (after lunch you have coffee in the lounge and browse through newspapers). There is, of course, the famous British tea at 3 p.m.—tea, cakes and biscuits served on elegant silver. Bani could not join in any of these. She would, if she did not eat in the apartment, buy her lunch from Oxford's 'covered market', and eat in my office. For American visitors, this put a strain on their domestic peace.

I enjoyed reading in the college lounge where there were lots of newspapers and magazines. After dinner, I would borrow books from the college reading room—generally fiction. But most of my academic research was done on the top floor of the Bodelian Library, which houses the India-related (and Sanskrit-related) books. Slowly, the book to appear ten years later as *Reason and Tradition in Indian Thought* was taking shape.

I did not have much to do with Oxford philosophy. All Souls' only philosophy fellow was Derek Parfit (still a junior fellow who was too shy to talk, and also was busy finishing his famous book on persons, which led to his election to a senior permanent fellowship a couple of years later). Michael Dummett, who had been a Fellow for a long time, had moved to New College with a professorship. Since I was working on Frege and Husserl, it was natural that I looked him up. We forged a friendship which I enjoyed; I attended his lectures, and he learned Husserl from me. As a matter of fact, Dummett began an intensive study of Husserl's works, resulting in various articles he wrote during the next few years.

I had always been an admirer of Peter Strawson and had taught his book, *Individuals*, to graduate classes in Calcutta and Oklahoma. Bimal had told me of Strawson's genuine love for India, so I looked him up at the Magdalene College. He took me out for lunch and we talked about matters of common interest. I sat in his Kant seminar and attended his lectures. Somewhat bland and boring as a lecturer, the sheer goodness of his personality compensated for his lack of charisma. I knew his ideas only too well, and there was nothing new that I found either in his seminars or in his lectures. On the other hand, Dummett, who at times spoke freely, and at other times thought aloud, I found exciting and challenging.

I also looked up George Holmes, an old friend from my Göttingen student days—now a well-known historian and a Fellow of St Catherine's. He had gone to Göttingen, after an Oxford degree, to study history, and, like me, lived in the *Historisches Colloquium*. Both of us tried hard to speak German well, although it would have been more convenient for us to speak in English. We caught up on the news about the German historians who had been graduate students at the *Colloquium*. Many of them had made their mark—Schulin, Kamp, Lieppelt, Schramm (the younger one), and a host of others.

On the whole, I enjoyed Oxford—walking on its streets by the famed colleges, sometimes walking along the Thames, visiting the bookshops, especially Blackwell's, and working in Bodelian's hallowed halls. Among old friends, besides Matilal, whom I saw almost every day, I renewed my acquaintance with Tapan Roy Choudhury and Amartya Sen. Young students from India would stop by, and so did American and German philosophers who were passing through.

I spent three terms at Oxford. Bani lived there for only one term. Chris de Linde came to see us from Paris—we had him as a guest for dinner at All Souls, which pleased him a great deal. We also took the usual tours around England. The beauty of England's countryside, especially of the Cotswold area (from where the stones that All Souls was built with were quarried) deeply inspired me.

II

About ten years later, in 1994, with the Humboldt Research Prize, I decided to spend the summer in Freiburg, Germany. Freiburg is very different from Oxford. The University in Oxford is older than the one at Freiburg by almost a hundred years. I believe Oxford's contribution to learning is incomparable—her only rival in Europe could be Paris. Oxford is more urbane—a large city compared even to its other rival in England, namely, Cambridge. Oxford's stately baroque mansions which house its thirty-odd colleges already constitute a remarkable skyline along the Thames. Freiburg, a lovely little town, is ensconced within the Black Forest. It also has a long history—a tower in the city centre memorializes witch burning, as does the Carfax in Oxford. Freiburg's contribution to Catholic theology rivals Oxford's contribution to Anglican and Protestant theology. Freiburg has, like Oxford, a tradition of historical research. While Oxford philosophy goes back, leaving aside

Edmund Husserl
(*Photo Courtesy of Herbert Spiegelberg*)

the middle ages, to John Locke, Freiburg's philosophy is much more recent but nevertheless has had its glory. The glorious period began with the Neo-Kantians (with Heinrich Rickert at the apex). Husserl moved there from Göttingen in 1916. Heidegger succeeded him in 1929. This brief period of about 23 years (Husserl died in 1939) falls squarely within my research interest, so where else could I wish to be—after Göttingen?

The people at the Husserl Archive, especially Hans Reiner Sepp (a young and amiable scholar), and Sigfried Rombach (then assistant to the Director and now at the University of Cologne), had arranged a one-room studio apartment for me above an inn with the name *Zur Trotte* (with the painted form of a rooster hanging out of the roof), situated in the heart of the town, on *Fischerau*, a romantic cobbled street. As the name suggests, the street was originally inhabited by fishermen. A canal, whose waters flow down the hill, ran parallel to the street. From my apartment, I could always hear the sound of the water flowing. On summer evenings, tourists as well as romantic couples would prom-enade on the cobbled street and crowd into the inn downstairs for drinks. A two-minute walk brings one to the city centre, where a column memorializes medieval witch-burning. Next to it, by a curious and ironical contrast, stands the arch of McDonalds. Tiny canals flow alongside every city street. I believe they are all man-made, to imitate Venice. The water is clean—it flows from a natural stream in the hills, around and into the river Dreisam, which divides the city into two.

Husserl's house on Loreto Strasse was, of course, the first place I visited—it was for me a pilgrimage. The present owner and inhabitant is a Professor of the History of Art at the University—a dignified and courteous person who has become accustomed to the chore of receiving visitors from countries around the world who come to see the Master's (as he puts it) residence. He points out, with distinct pride, where the Master studied, relaxed to smoke his pipe (Husserl's last illness was emphysema), where he received visitors, where the maids were admit-ted by the gracious Frau Malvine, and so forth. The old furniture is not there but the bookshelves still are. Then there is the path along which the Master set out on his evening walks, crossing the street into Loreto Hill's winding upward rise. I could imagine him resting on his walking stick as a support, stopping to settle a point at issue with his young assistant, Martin Heidegger. My imagination brought in the more well-known visitors to the house, including Eugen Fink, Hans Lipps, Edith Stein, Roman Ingarden (returning from Poland), Alfred Schutz and Fritz Kaufmann (visiting from Vienna), Dorion Cairns from Harvard, and many others.

Husserl's Tombstone

Husserl had to move from the Loreto Strasse apartment soon after retirement. He did not have the financial means to pay for such a spacious place. (His savings were meager, and the money he had put into the Göttingen house was all lost with the devaluation of war bonds after the First World War.) He moved to a more modest place, Schöne Ecke 6, the apartment where he died some years later.

The picture of his death, which I reconstructed from stories and recollections (especially of a ninety-year-old Catholic nun, still alive, who stayed by his bedside, day after day, and persuaded the Catholic church to agree to bury him—inspite of the persecution of the Nazis against non-Aryans—just outside the church walls, within the church precinct) was tragic, moving but nonetheless inspiring. I could not help but contrast Husserl's predicament with that of Heidegger, whom Husserl chose as his successor but who collaborated with the Nazis, and, as the Rector of Freiburg, signed an order depriving Husserl of all privileges of using the University facilities. Until his death, Heidegger did not express any regret for his Nazi past but tried to explain it away with all sorts of obfuscating jargon.

I also visited all those little Black Forest villages in the vicinity of Freiburg where Husserl retired during the holidays to write. That added to the charm of the Black Forest. The young philosopher Rombach drove me around in his tiny Volkswagen. This young man hailed from the region, with deep roots in the area. He took me to a small rural museum depicting farmers' lives over the centuries, and pointed out a tiny wooden rocker where, on his (and the museum guide's) account, his mother had slept when she was a tiny baby!

My work on Husserl's papers in the Archive continued. It involved long hours of reading from the voluminous manuscripts he had left behind. The story of this Archive is worth telling. As Husserl was being severely humiliated by the Nazis, a former student, Father van Breda, a Belgian Carmelite priest, visited him in Freiburg with the request to let him (van Breda) remove Husserl's library and all of his papers to Belgium, in order to save them from possible destruction. Van Breda sent the papers through the Belgian Embassy in Berlin in diplomatic bags over a period of time. After the war, the Rockefeller Foundation and UNESCO funded the Archive. Scholars—especially those who had once worked with Husserl, and who could decipher the Gabelsberger stenography in which Husserl wrote—were appointed to transcribe the Nachlass manuscripts into typescripts. Slowly, a whole series of *Husserliana* appeared. One of the greatest satisfactions of my life lies in having been connected with this process.

I especially loved to read the old man's manuscripts. It appears that the philosopher thought while he was writing. He was always asking new questions, criticizing his old positions, seeking to find new ways out. I was thrilled as I went on reading the manuscripts of his declining years—years not only of growing physical debility but of great disappointment and humiliation. How odd, he wonders, that he who had devoted his life to the renewal of German philosophy, and lost a son for the 'Fatherland' in the First World War, was declared by ignorant 'bums' (of the SS) as unfit to be a true German? Even close students stopped visiting him. On one of his birthdays, very few people sent cards—he wrote to Hans Lipps and thanked him for having sent one. But he did not abandon his search for a 'true foundation' for scientific knowledge, and refused to accept the irrationalism of emerging 'existential' thinking. I was inspired.

My project to work out a *Gesamtdarstellung* of this man's philosophy became clearer, and I found it not only philosophically interesting but also personally inspiring. Lester Ebree and Günther Patzig encouraged me by saying, 'If you don't do it, nobody else in the world could'.

The City of Brotherly Love

Returning from New York, I lived in Norman, Oklahoma, for seven years. The thought of leaving Oklahoma again never occurred to me. The house was comfortable, Padmini was growing up with us, Mitti had finished Law School, and had joined a law firm. The climate suited us well; the Indian community with whom we generally socialized was congenial. My writing was going well. My research money allowed me to go to conferences and visit libraries in case I needed to do so. The Department provided me with all that I needed for my work, and I got a great deal of respect from the campus community.

Most unexpectedly one afternoon, I received a phone call from Joe Margolis, asking me to consider moving to Philadelphia to join the Temple University faculty. At first I dismissed the idea but as I thought about it, it seemed to take hold of me. Earlier on, I had declined invitations to the Northwestern University in Evanston, Illinois, and the University of Hawaii in Honolulu; refused to apply to Yale even after being requested to do so by Ruth Marcus, who dominated Yale's department; and left the New School too. So why consider a move to Philadelphia? Sometimes you do not discover the deep truth about your psyche until you are awakened from a 'dogmatic slumber'. I was surprised to discover that I had lived in Oklahoma too long, that my mind was pining for a more intellectual climate, offering more challenge to my ideas. The ideas that New School had occasioned had been written down, and had earned for me some recognition. But what next? I decided to accept the invitation. Bani would stay in Norman for some time to take care of Padmini. I found a flat in Chestnut Hill on the edge of Philadelphia, and joined the faculty of Temple in the autumn of '85.

Temple University is located in North Philadelphia on Broad Street, about two miles north of the City Hall. The neighbourhood is notorious for its crime rate; so also is the area surrounding the more prestigious University of Pennsylvania. That is no consolation as far as Temple is concerned but as the taxi driver who first brought me to the Temple campus said, 'They would say bad things about Temple's neighbourhood, but not about the University of Pennsylvania.' As a matter of fact, all the great urban universities in the USA have been victims of the same urban malignancy—Columbia, Chicago, and UCLA. Yale's New Haven and Harvard's Cambridge are no better as towns. Crimes and drugs stalk you everywhere. In that regard, Temple is no exception. But Temple, I think, has a rapport with the surrounding ghettos, since more young people from them attend Temple than is possible in the case of the more prestigious and expensive schools named above. Originally a Baptist Institution (which accounts for the name), now it belongs to the Commonwealth System of Universities of the state of Pennsylvania, and the name is no more descriptive of the University. While its undergraduate students are largely drawn from the sprawling urban area around it, the graduate school is selective and of high quality. The Philosophy Department has a good reputation. I came as the replacement of Monroe Beardsley—quite a famous philosopher, and arguably America's most famous scholar in aesthetics.

The city of Philadelphia ('Brotherly Love') is a historic city, where America's constitution was adopted and freedom declared. It remained the capital of the United States until Washington was built on the Potomac. Battlefields of the American War of Independence almost surround the city—Germantown and Valley Forge, Trenton and Princeton, to name the cities of the more famous battles. The city stretches along the Delaware River, which separates it from New Jersey, and is divided into two by the Schulkyll River, which runs through it into the Delaware River. The centre of the city, originally a colonial area, where red brick colonial houses (now restored), attract wealthy yuppies to return from the suburb, bear testimony to the original Philadelphia, where its most famous citizen, Benjamin Franklin, lived and worked. North of the old city is the part which Franklin, when Ambassador in Paris, had Munchausen (the architect of modern Paris) design after Paris; the spacious Franklin Parkway leads up to the magnificent art museum (imitating the Champs Elysse leading up to the Louvre). The most European of all American cities, with numerous impressive statues, bridges over the Schulkyll, monuments, public statues, and a park, the Fairmount Park, running for tens of miles into the heart of the city—all this magnificence fills my heart with joy. But it is surrounded by poverty, ghettos, crime, and homelessness, and one often wonders if the city of 'brotherly love' is not also the city of crime and all that goes with it.

Initially we rented a town house in the north-west part of the city, Chestnut Hill—perhaps the city's most wealthy section, dotted with superb eighteenth-century mansions. But soon we moved farther away from the city to the small community of Ambler. Padmini moved in with us to go to a High School—one of the few Girls' Schools left—in Chestnut Hill, the Springside School. And for three years I drove her to and from school, followed her work and progress, and got to know, for the first time, the pleasures and the pains of parenting a high school student in this country—which also meant getting to know young people of an age group with whom I had very little acquaintance before. Without Padmini, our lives would have been spent without much of its pleasures, and also many of its challenges. Her company has been a source of delight, which brings with it its own counterpoints, but every moment was precious.

Life in Philadelphia presented a rich variety of intellectual diet. The city has, besides Temple, several distinguished institutions of higher education—the University of Pennsylvania, and the three Quaker colleges: Swarthmore, Bryn Mawr, and Haverford. Their libraries, faculty, and students offered many hitherto unknown possibilities. Princeton is an hour's drive away, and it was possible to go for meetings to all these superb academic institutions. For some years I worked on Gödel's papers on Husserl in the Princeton Library. But the most rewarding was the Penn library, its holdings on Sanskrit proving to be an invaluable asset for me, compensating for the distance from the Calcutta Sanskrit College and the Bodelian, and making it possible to bring *Reason and Tradition* to an end in 1990, and make progress on the second part of the Indian philosophy project.

At Temple, Joe Margolis proved to be an extremely valuable colleague. Being himself one of the country's most distinguished philosophers, Margolis's total dedication to philosophical thinking and writing is overwhelming. Invariably courteous and highly sophisticated, Margolis continuously engaged me in philosophical dialogues, challenging my fundamental philosophical commitments in a manner that combined incisive criticism with gentle appreciation. Many of the papers I wrote during the decade at Temple bear the stamp of those conversations.

As in the New School, so also at Temple, I was lucky to have a group of bright graduate students. Like McKenna and Kirkland in New York, Michael Barnhart and Christina Schüs (from Germany) at Temple rewarded me by their creative and productive work. While Barnhart read

Husserl and Hegel in order to be able to appropriate Buddhist thought creatively, Schüs translated her deep concern with Husserl into a post-modernist feminist philosophy. I learnt from both. Just as at New School, where my interest turned to Hegel and historicism, at Temple I tried to respond to the post-modernist critique of phenomenology. But by now, I was beginning to realize that my work on Indian philosophy had to be brought to completion without further delay, for how can one ignore, at the age of sixty-five, the imminent possibility of death?

Our social life continued to be dominated by the Indian immigrant community but—in contrast with the Oklahoma years—now almost exclusively by the Bengalis. The Bengali community of Philadelphia and its surroundings, known as the Delaware Valley, is not large but is mid-sized, closely knit, group-connected, as much by friendships as by conflicts and quarrels. With my knowledge of Bengali culture and past association with Calcutta's academia and intellectual life (and, of course, Bani's heritage), we were naturally drawn towards this group as much as this group was towards us. I was elected President of the Bengali Cultural association, known as *Pragati* (progress), in which capacity I had to oversee the annual celebration of the various *Pujas* (chiefly of Durga, the beautiful goddess with ten arms, standing on a lion, and killing with a spear, a green-bodied demon who was reportedly threatening all living beings on earth, and even the gods in heaven), also arrange for picnics and 'cultural functions' with artists visiting from Calcutta. During such Puja celebrations and cultural functions, I, as the President of the organization, found myself in the inevitable position of mediating conflicts and, much in the Gandhian fashion, keeping the lavatories clean, and the rented halls 'in order', after the audience were gone. One is impressed by how people come to a foreign country with most of their habits and manners intact—they are carefully hidden when dealing with Americans, but erupt and come to the fore when among their kind. Perhaps this is how it should be, and this is why there is such a mushroom growth of ethnic 'cultural' societies.

Every Indian community, organized mainly according to linguistic groups, is proud of its culture. Celebration of its 'cultural heritage' takes the form of songs and dances, musicals and dramas, food and dress, as members of the community had known or experienced that heritage while in their country 'back home'—for which there is an understandable feeling of nostalgia. The community's aim is as much to relive those experiences as to provide occasions for the young generation to 'learn' and assimilate their culture. The older people, who have grown up being a part of that culture, think they understand it all. The younger generation—born and brought up in America—are confused by the strange sights and sounds, not knowing the myths and legends, and prefer to settle for the food and drinks, games and sports of their new country. There is a certain naivety regarding all this on the part of the older generation, who assume that they already know it all but whose 'understanding' is more often than not shallow and false—and it is a case of the blind leading the blind. The supreme motivation, of course, is to prevent the children from 'becoming Americans', from dating and marrying Americans, and to ensure that they remain Indians (Bengali, Oriya, or whatever the case may be). Underneath the Western clothing and manners, there is an almost unavoidable sense of guilt on the part of immigrant parents, that they have brought with them their children, who have been 'thrown to the wolves', and the exciting life of the USA. All that moral 'degradation' can be tolerated if the child goes to an Ivy League college, and can eventually become a doctor.

The memorable events of my Philadelphia years are: an invitation to be the President of the Indian Philosophical Congress (1986); arranging, as the President of the Bengali Cultural Association, the celebrations of the Tricentenary of Calcutta; being awarded the Humboldt Research Prize from Germany (1992); and Padmini's graduation from high school and her going to Bryn Mawr College (1994).

I was told I was the first person living and teaching in a foreign country to be elected the President of the Indian Philosophical Congress. This was to me a matter of satisfaction—learning that the Philosophical community still remembered me and valued my work. I went to Calcutta, where the annual meetings were held that year, somewhat more appropriately for me to preside over. My Presidential address was devoted to examining and re-interpreting the thesis of *śabdapramāṇa*. I noticed that I had changed my views on this matter. I met many philosophers from all over India, especially many younger scholars whom I had not known before. If only I could set aside the questions regarding the quality of the work being done! I was overwhelmed by love and affection, and, for a brief time, realized rather poignantly, what I had missed for so long by living outside the country.

Returning to Philadelphia, I devoted myself—under the leadership of Krishna Lahiri—to organizing the Tricentennial celebrations of the city of Calcutta. This was an act of sheer love and gratitude for the city to which I owe so much. My inaugural lecture, in Haverford College, moved some to tears, because I could not help being personal, referring to 'a sixteen-year-old boy from the neighbouring state of Orissa coming to Calcutta, carrying an insatiable curiosity to learn and to make friends, and immediately falling in love with the city'. We set up an exhibition at Haverford, devoted to Calcutta's cultural history. For me, the most romantic part of it was an exhibition of documents borrowed from the Maritime Museum (all about two hundred years of trade between Calcutta and Philadelphia), of which the central personality was a Calcutta merchant of the name of Ram Dulal Dey, whom the Philadelphia merchants simply adored. Mayor Goode declared the month 'Calcutta month'. I felt proud.

The award of the Humboldt Research Prize for 1992 meant for me that the German scholars eventually recognized the value of my life-long research on German philosophy, especially on Husserl's phenomenology. The money allowed me to set aside a small fund for social work in Orissa, and to use the rest for visits to Germany, for research and writing—resulting in extended visits, on successive summers, to Göttingen, Freiburg, and Tübingen. I must say I enjoyed living in those picture-postcard towns more than meeting the scholars who lived there (with the sole exception of my dear old friend Günther Patzig in Göttingen).

Padmini finished at Springside, and went up to Bryn Mawr—a lovely campus of imitation Oxford-style buildings and greens. I had for so long carefully guarded her and protected her; now she could go her own way, making her own choices. The thought was as exhilarating as painful. I would drive up to Bryn Mawr—a distance of 20 miles—once a week to see her. This led to a deepening of my friendship with Michael Krausz, who had, in the meantime, developed a strong emotional tie for India, having been involved in saving the ecology of the Doabs and Ladakh, and captured by the sheer beauty of Ladakh and the Kulu Valley.

Visits to India

There are two kinds of immigrants. There are those who are forced out of their native lands by poverty, starvation or political persecution; they leave for their survival. And there are those who immigrate for better opportunities than what their native land could offer, for a better future, with a dream in their hearts. I certainly, and, I believe most immigrants from the Indian sub-continent, do not belong to the first group. I would then fall in the second group. But do I? I think, there must be another class of immigrants to which I belong, for like many others, I did not come to the United States in order to immigrate. I came with a 'green card', to be sure, but that is because the University of Oklahoma required me to get it before they could offer me a tenured position. They did the paper work, and I collected the card in Calcutta. But I did not perceive myself to be an immigrant; we were not 'migrating', leaving our homeland and settling down in our new, adopted country. I thought that I was just going to the USA with a professorship, still on leave from the University of Calcutta—if possible, to do some research, which I could not do in India; to put the children through school there, possibly for a better education (not knowing in which way it would be better), and eventually, not too long afterwards, to return to India! But slowly and imperceptibly, while the thought of returning burns within your heart, the flame becomes a flicker, and you find that dream—now the dream of returning—being deferred to a distant future. Unknowingly, not as a result of conscious thought, a reversal takes place. You still must return. Despite all your professional achievements, despite the money you make, and the future of your family, the idea of return provides the only eschatological meaning to your existence. At this point, all two (or three) kinds of immigrants are as one—or, I would suppose, most of them are. The original dream of the new land of opportunities is displaced by the dream of return from the 'Diaspora'. The fate of the Jews is the fate of all immigrants.

Before that dream is realized at the end of your lifetime, the best you can do is to visit the home country as often as you can. Those visits replace the periodical re-enactment of the original myths surrounding the 'Diaspora'. You return but not finally. You return with a sense of guilt for having left the land, for not being by the side of the people who had placed their trust in you. You have to tell them that you still exist, that you still have your country in your heart, and her tradition in your mind, and that it is only a question of time before you return.

Does the country really need you? An Indian diplomat in New York, whom I knew in Presidency College, in the course of a conversation, learnt that I had become a philosopher, and remarked that India could afford to do without philosophers—meaning, what the country needed were scientists, engineers, and doctors. As a contrast, take the view of Sachin Ganguly—a most remarkable young philosopher in Calcutta, whose life was cut short in an untimely manner—who once remarked to me, 'Jiten-da, I do not believe in what is called brain drain. Those who have left should have left. The country is all the better ('lighter' as he put it) for their departure. We have enough people here at home'. Sachin perhaps meant that those who believe in India are the ones on whom the country can depend, not those who are fortune seekers in foreign lands. To believe that the country needs all those Indians who crowd in on commuter trains to New York City, is to attach to them an importance which they do not deserve. (Later on, the country welcomed their dollars, not them.)

Fair enough. One has to maintain a low key when visiting India. Do not show off your newly acquired wealth (India has far wealthier persons, you will be told). Do not talk about your three-bedroom, two-car garage home, your cars, and all the electronic gadgets that make life easier. The fact is, the typical immigrant understands neither Indian culture nor Western culture. He is ever moved by the newly found gold (in whatever quantity); if he is a scientist, in the opportunities for scientific research; if a technologist, he is overwhelmed by the idea of not merely using technology but of contributing to its development. Typically, to find solace in some deep recess of his heart, he turns to religion. Temples are springing up all over America. Men who never visited a temple, and who professed indifference to religion while living in India, now go to temples, sing Bhajans, and perform rituals. Many will still not admit to themselves that they have had a change of heart, a 'conversion'. They will say that they were doing it for the sake of the children, or because 'going back to one's roots' is fashionable. The same people, when visiting India, in Calcutta, Delhi or Bombay, visit five-star hotels to take their friends out for drinks—but not for them the holy men, the pilgrimages, the temples, unless, again, it is for their children's sake!

There were, up until 1989, two fixtures during my visits to India—my mother and Calcutta. With her gone, Calcutta remains—Calcutta, with her teeming millions, filth on the streets, automobile fumes, chaos on the roads, poverty in the slums, and so forth. At first I stayed with Tara Chatterjee in their spacious Ballygunje home. A former pupil at the University, Tara drew me into her family and found for me a niche alongside her husband and four children. I felt at home. Then Swami Lokeswarananda, with his dignified, quiet demeanour and unobtrusive hospitality, made me feel at home in the spacious well-maintained premises of the Rama Krishna Mission Institute (RKMI). I began giving lectures at the RKMI on sundry themes, every time I lived there, and the Swami treated me as a guest, not accepting any fees from me for lodging and meals. My lectures, held at the Sivananda Hall, were generally well attended, but I was never sure how many understood what I talked about. I began to notice that the lectures in Calcutta were taking a different shape from the scientific papers I presented in USA and Europe. In the West, the papers were what one would call 'professional', 'scholarly' and 'scientific'. The Calcutta lectures were composed in Calcutta. Without the help of libraries, they were motivated by more 'practical' and broad-based concerns and interests. In a certain way, the two were complementary. But I had always suspected what a dear friend of mine called 'sagery'. Am I falling prey to that temptation? But a merely scholarly, 'scientific' philosophy had never captured my mind. The old interests of my youth—Gandhi and Sri Aurobindo—were not totally gone. Like Kant, I continued to believe that philosophy had to be, in spite of its scientific character, a theory of *Welt Weisheit* and Husserl's idea that the philosopher has to be a 'functionary' of humankind did not cease to appeal to me. How to keep the two side at harmony? The Calcutta lectures were inspired by this sense of harmony. They did not quite succeed. I did not lecture in Calcutta to be recognized. I wanted to tell my friends what and how I was thinking. I was returning their friendship. This was the place I had grown up in, where I had learnt philosophy, where I had forged lasting friendships and imbibed a sensitivity to human values. I wanted to generate conversations, and feel I was still a part of that community of minds. In this I was successful; the measure of this success was simple—my own joy.

In 1995, the University of Jadavpur honoured me by conferring a doctorate *honoris causa*, on me. It has amazed me how Jadavpur had come closer to me than my alma mater, the University of Calcutta. I seldom visit the latter. College Square is just too far from the RKMI; the department has moved to a new building in Alipore, and the faculty made me feel that I had abandoned them. Jadavpur University, on the other hand, is closer to the RKMI, and Debi Prasad Chattopadhyaya and Pranab Sen—two members of the Jadavpur Philosophy Department—are interested in my thinking. Sukharanjan Saha and Prodyot Mukherjee do Indian philosophy to my liking, Krishna Roy and Chhanda Gupta have become like members of my family. I became close to them and am touched by their love. Jadavpur's decision to confer the doctorate on me came as a surprise. I was neither their student, nor had I ever been a member of their faculty. Bani had a degree from there, so there was a family connection. But I had been visiting them and lecturing in the department for at least ten years. I accepted the honour with thanks.

The news reached Orissa. I received a telephone call from the Vice-chancellor of the Utkal University at Bhubaneswar, Orissa, from where, he said, I should have received such an honour first. Wasn't I a son of Orissa? They regretted that they were not the first (actually Burdwan University had conferred an honourary D.Litt. on me nearly ten years earlier). But could Bani and I visit them as the University's guests, and let the University Community honour me in some befitting manner? I agreed. For the first time, we were not staying at home in Orissa. We arrived at the Bhubaneswar railway station and were driven straight to the University's Guest House. For the first time, newspaper men, TV reporters, literary critics, student representatives (and, of course, University faculty) kept me busy, reminding me that I was Oriya first and foremost, a nephew of the Chaudhury brothers and, of course, about my father and brother. I reassured them of my love for Orissa. Only, the Orissa I knew, where I always returned was my village—not the new middle-class that had arisen since I left the state.

In a way, the same is true of India as a whole, including Calcutta. Within the past three decades, India has changed. A highly sophisti-cated, westernized (rather, Americanized) middle-class has come into being. They drink and dance at parties, even birthday parties. Young people talk about Michael Jackson and the rest of the avant garde musicians. Families in Delhi and Bombay go to Hong Kong, Singapore, London and New York for vacations and shopping. Young intellectuals practise (or rather talk about) deconstruction. Gandhi is regarded as having pushed the country back. Those who combine their westernization with *Hindutva* politics wish, and announce publicly, that it would have been better if Godse had eliminated Gandhi earlier. Others—liberal in politics—wish Gandhi's antiquated ideas about technology had not postponed the entrance of 'high-tech' into India. Even in Calcutta—where as students, and later as University teachers, we revelled in liberal socialist politics trying to combine Gandhi and Marx—I heard young students tell me that the BJP was showing the way: bring back the ideology of *Hindutva*. I shivered within myself, in disbelief and fear of the unknown. (The ideologists of *Hindutva* were not believers in Hinduism.)

Added to these changes is the report (I have heard about this) that, even in Calcutta, young people are indulging in drugs. I refuse to believe it. I cling to the Calcutta we left three decades ago—the picture of the city we have lovingly protected.

The more India becomes westernized, the more do I seem to slip back to the India that I adore and refuse to concede is no more. More and more I get interested in Sanskrit philosophical tradition and refuse to have anything to do with the 'high-tech' invasion. I tend to cling to the Gandhian village-centred India, even if it is possible that that India never existed, or ever will—but what a romantic picture! What is amazing is that my annual visits to India during the last thirty years have not been able to delete that picture. Maybe I have a genuine dream, a way of looking at things, which is worth preserving.

For a thinker, the most powerful move—despite the practical weakness of thinking—is interpretation. All my efforts have been focused upon reinterpreting Indian thought.

Philosophical Journey, Roots, and Religion

As far as I can recollect, I cannot identify any particular experience which led to a lifelong concern with philosophy. High school dabbling in philosophy books did not create any interest to pursue the subject. Those were the years the Indian freedom movement was coming to an inspiring climax. Within the family, one uncle and his wife were Gandhians, another with his wife, was a Marxist. The one intellectual issue which, in a few years, would mature into my first philosophical concern, was 'Gandhi vs. Marx', also a narrower question regarding the effectiveness and desirability of non-violence as a method for winning freedom. Another author whom I began reading during my first year in college still muddied the field: this was Sri Aurobindo. What attracted me to Aurobindo was not so much his reputation as a *yogin*, or even as a scholar, but his role in the Indian freedom movement prior to Gandhi's entrance into Indian politics. Aurobindo's brother, Barin Ghose, was, of course, a leader of the terrorist anti-British movement that sprang up in Bengal after the partition of Bengal. So I took Aurobindo to be of the same political camp, and wondered whether Gandhi's leadership was good for India. Slowly, as I read more of Aurobindo's dauntingly difficult books. I became fascinated by his efforts to construct a grand metaphysical system, particularly by his claims to have refuted and overcome Samkara's *māyāvāda*. By the time I arrived in Calcutta to study at Presidency College, two philosophical questions had gripped my mind—'Gandhi vs. Marx' and 'Sri Aurobindo vs. Samkara'. With regard to the former, I leaned towards Gandhi, and although I read Marx's major philosophical works, I never was a Marxist. Most of my friends at Presidency College were Marxists, and in order to be able to converse and argue with them I had to be conversant with Marx's writings. It was much later, during my New York days, that I began to appreciate an aspect of Marx's thought which I had been blind to—namely, that characterizing Marx solely in terms of materialism is missing an important part of it. When human labour shapes history, that labour is as spiritual and intentional as thoughts are. I got over my early worry about historical materialism vis-a-vis the constitutive power of thoughts. The other concern I had, during those early college years, was about the role of individuals in history. Plekhanov's essay on the topic did not satisfy me. I had to read Hegel's work in order to appreciate the depths of Marx's thinking. While my understanding of Marx deepened, I began to detach the Marx I understood from Engels, and also from Lenin. Marxism's opposition to Gandhi remained, and I felt myself always on the Mahatma's side in the long run, insofar as an individual could resist the force of *Zeitgeist.* Tagore's poem '*ekla chalo, ekla chalo*' (Let us go alone), a favourite of the Mahatma, has a strong appeal.

The other philosophical concern of the Presidency College years was: is the world, along with finite individuals, merely a false appearance as Samkara would have it, or is it a real manifestation of an essential aspect of *brahman*, a self-differentiation by virtue of the *brahman's* own creative energy, as Aurobindo would have it? I came to college, already with a prejudice in favour of Aurobindo, and in spite of an intense effort, which continued for the entire four years of college in Calcutta, to read and understand Samkara, I found myself unable to appreciate the *māyāvāda*. I came to know that the world, in Samkara's view, was not non-existent, that Samkara introduced a new category—'not describable as either existent or non-existent', that the *brahman*, as pure consciousness, was the foundation of all phenomena, but in spite of all these, it appeared to me unconvincing that *māyā*, not as the *brahman's* creative power, but as a cosmic Ignorance that was not rooted in the *brahman's* own nature, could conceal and distort the nature of the one reality that is all there is. The dualism between the *brahman* and *avidyā* seemed to be hardly compatible with a non-dualistic philosophy, and the anxiety, that if ignorance could succeed in concealing the *brahman*, what could be so powerful as to be able to remove that concealment seemed very tantalizing. The use of the rope-snake illusion, I suspected, was most inappropriate to understand the metaphysical situation of the *brahman*-world illusion.

Of the two problems that haunted me during my college years, I had no doubt about the intrinsic superiority of the Gandhian philosophy—

although at that time, the skeletons in the closet of Russian socialism had not yet been disclosed, and stories about Stalin's numberless victims and mock trials were still regarded by my Marxist friends as being no better than capitalist propaganda (a convenient self-deception).

It was at this time that I was introduced to the theory of knowledge on the one hand, and Navya-Nyāya logic on the other. With my proclivity for analytical thinking, both provided fields where I could exercise that ability, and as I enjoyed the Kantian epistemology and the Navya-Nyāya theory of *pramāṇa*, those earlier problems, still unsolved to my satisfaction, slowly receded to the background, like the outlines of a country whose shores you leave as your ship sails away. My philosophical interests changed, became more emancipated from the political and eschatological motives of my earlier concerns. They became more theoretical.

II

Two new questions began to monopolize my thoughts. At Göttingen, mathematical pursuits raised the spectre of Platonism. Reading Whitehead and Husserl's *Logical Investigations* led me to believe in abstract entities such as propositions, numbers, and sets. In Calcutta, I had devoted some time to reading Plato's dialogues, and my admiration for Platonic metaphysics was strengthened. At the same time, I became aware of the growing anti-Platonism of analytic thinkers in England and America. Frege, Russell, and Whitehead were gone; they had been replaced by a generation of their disciples—Carnap, Quine, and Ryle, disciples who sought to 'preserve' the heritage of their Masters by annihilating their philosophies and replacing them with their own. I began to ask myself; can Platonism be defended—and, for that purpose, if necessary, be suitably amended—against its vociferous critics? The critic of Platonism to whom I wanted to respond was the logical empiricist, who distrusted, on grounds of his empiricism, all abstract, nontangible, non-sensuous entities. The critic of Platonism who raised his head after two or so decades was not the empiricist, but the historicist, who thought of essences—typically Platonic entities—as ahistorical, and so, having no place, except as a provisional construct in his historicized scheme of things. Was this criticism justified against a Frege, a Whitehead, and a Husserl?

The phenomenology of Husserl confronted me with another enduring question in philosophy. Phenomenology asks us to focus on the way things are presented in consciousness, on the meanings that things have for those experiencing consciousness. Understanding consciousness as intentional and meaning-giving, phenomenology raised consciousness, in its transcendental (i.e., world-constituting) role, as the foundational principle for philosophy. While this was going on in Germany, Wittgenstein was glorifying language—at first, in the *Tractatus*, as an ideal system of mirroring the structure of reality; then as language-games which we play, and within whose public rules meanings are constituted—at the expense of the alleged privacy of consciousness. Returning from Göttingen to India, and embarking upon a long career of teaching philosophy, I jumped headlong into the controversy: *'consciousness'* or *'language'*? Very slowly but steadily, I explored many different aspects and dimensions of this question. Is not 'consciousness' itself a word having its original home in a language-game? Is not language—primarily as the act of speaking—a modality of consciousness? Cannot the first reduction come under the scope of the second reduction? At the same time, is it possible that in each of the two reductions—of consciousness to language as well as of language to consciousness—there is a surplus of what is sought to be reduced, and so a failure of the project? When consciousness is situated within a language-game, there is an *awareness* of it being so situated; when language is reduced to consciousness of speaking, the history of language, its diachronic aspect, escapes the presence to consciousness. If, in response, language be regarded not alone as *la parle* but also as *la langue,* consciousness must likewise be expanded beyond the limits of the transparency of the present—into the deep recesses of memory, and the indefinite anticipation of the not-yet. Linguistic meaning and the meanings things have for consciousness seem to be but two aspects of one and the same discourse. But is not the very reduction of language to speech at fault, for is it not necessary for a language that it must have a material corporeality? Yet what is this materiality of language but the corporeality of consciousness as bodily? This dialogue went on until 'consciousness' proved to be the more all-comprehensive category, and language, despite its irrepressibility, seemed to have been overcome in the silence of the ineffable. There is another line of speculation which I pursued, and which I suggested in the course of a lecture on the 'Root of Twentieth-century Philosophy' in the World Congress of Philosophy in Boston—are not consciousness and language both unified in a third something? It is Heidegger's *Dasein* or is it Hegel's *Geist*? Asking this question shows that I was already caught up with Hegel and Heidegger. The path of thinking had become enormously more complicated than the simplistic formulation the alternatives might suggest.

This complication is due to the added dimension of Indian philosophy, which accompanied my thinking, even when it was not the theme, as unfailingly as a shadowy presence. Curiously enough, the relationship was often reversed—when Indian philosophy became the focus and the theme, Husserl and phenomenology functioned as an unfailing shadowy presence. Consider the two philosophical concerns to which I have devoted the preceding few pages: 'Platonism vs. anti-Platonism', and 'consciousness vs. language'. As I pursued these issues in the context of Western philosophy, how could I not turn to, and learn from, the rich tradition of Indian thinking? Buddhism was on the anti-Platonic side, whereas the grammarians posited abstract meaning-entities (*sphoṭas*), and the Navya-Naiyāyikas revelled in using abstract entities of all hues and colours. The non-dualistic Vedanta made consciousness (*cit*) foundational, but, to be sure, a consciousness that is non-intentional (*nirviṣaya*), and non-egological (*nirāśraya*). The Grammarian Bhartṛhari would not have any consciousness that is not interwoven with language, the two domains being, in the long run, non-different.

My philosophical journey has been as much through the Occident as through the Orient. There have been many sub-paths which I have tried, and then shunned. One of them is called 'comparative philosophy'. The philosopher compares the East and the West (or, rather schools, figures, concepts, and theories from the East with those from the West). This project never attracted me, for—among other reasons—I could not decide where I should situate myself so that I could compare the two. I found no ground outside the East and the West. Another sub-path was to borrow bits and pieces from the East, and from the West, and combine them to 'manufacture' what may be called 'World Philosophy'. The sheer artificiality of such a project repelled me, and the designation 'World Philosophy' seemed to me to be a misnomer. Thinking cannot simply put together ideas as though they are slabs of stone. Thinking has to enter into them, loosen their rigidity, transform them into the fluidity of its own movement, and refashion a new form out of that fluid, like the way a jeweller transforms an ornament into a new one. Moreover, the essence of philosophy lies not in the conclusions arrived at, in the theses and positions, in the systems constructed but rather in the *process* of thinking that leads up to them. Without that process, those conclusions are but corpses.

So I gave up the path which many of my predecessors in India had followed. Much of the work, for example, of Radhakrishnan left me cold, and I was bored to death. On the other hand, Aurobindo and K.C. Bhattacharya (and the latter's son Kalidas) showed me the way. I had to develop my thinking from within Indian philosophy, and my thinking, from within Western tradition, until they both mingled, and I could not distinguish what I was thinking about—the East or the West. Philosophizing would then become one process, all the richer for the diversity that goes into its formation, but nevertheless flowing smoothly, undisturbed by the externality of comparisons and of the 'putting together' of different traditions. That is the goal which I have pursued.

III

Within Western philosophy my interest still centres around Husserl and Kant, as it has for the past three decades or so. To think of Husserl is to think also of Heidegger. Heidegger has been Husserl's other, not from the outside but from within Husserl's thinking. The same is true of Kant —to think with Kant is to think of Hegel, who critiqued and opposed Kant from within.

'Husserl-Heidegger'—the caption designates not only two philosophers in their internal relation and contrast but also the whole story and tragedy of philosophy. The Master symbolized relentless pursuit of the path of thinking to its end, which—as in the case of Socrates's drinking poison—was 'dying to live'. Refusing to sacrifice his rationality in the face of the gathering clouds or irrationality in Europe, Husserl fell victim to the latter, suffered indignities and eventually, as he passed away, was buried outside a Catholic church's walls. The Master's self-anointed disciple and successor, glorifying irrationality over rational thinking, turned into an apologist for the perpetrators, and then sought to recant his mistake without owning up to it. Husserl's scrupulous adherence to the idea of thinking that he had set for himself impressed me, and for me, he ranked with Socrates as the main representative of the greatness of Western thinking. Heidegger was a great philosopher no doubt, but fell victim to a host of assorted irrationalisms—romantic nationalism, anti-rationalism, mystification of the Germanic tradition, and obfuscation of thought and expression. Although my natural inclination was not to take Heidegger seriously, Hannah Arendt persuaded me to overlook his personal failings and to learn to appreciate his important ideas. I imbibed from Heidegger his hermeneutic thinking and from Husserl the rigour of descriptive, scientific thinking. Much of my work during the eighties consisted of combining the two.

What Heidegger was to Husserl, Hegel was to Kant. The limits that Kant put on the human faculties of knowing, and their reach, were abolished by Hegel—thereby, in effect, abolishing the line of demarcation between man and God. This Vedantic strain had a subtle attraction for me, and I started reading and teaching Hegel's *Phenomenology*. At what point my Kantian sense of limits slowly gave way to a historical-developmental view of human cognition and morality, I do not know. I still taught Kant's *Critique of Pure Reason*, trying to make sense of the idea of human receptivity to what is given, independently of any inter-vention by thinking, as well as of the conception of moral law as a categorical imperative. But the Hegelian insight that the distinction between receptivity and spontaneity, the given and the constructed, is to be relativized to the level of discourse you are in, made sense as well. I could, to my satisfaction, identify the limits, perhaps excesses, of Hegelian thinking—two of them, most of all: his 'Eurocentricity' and his 'Absolutism'. I looked for a history of consciousness which has no closure, i.e., does not end in an Absolute knowing; I wanted to make room in my developmental account of the human spirit for more about African, Chinese, and Indian experiences. The idea of rewriting Hegel's *Phenomenology* became a passion but also one of those dreams every thinker has, knowing fully well that he cannot fulfil it. But such a 'regulative Idea' gives meaning to your being as a thinker.

It is with regard to this plan of rewriting the Hegelian text, that Husserl's later works seemed to be of momentous significance. Singu-larly free from Hegel's 'Absolutism', with a sense for the open-endedness of the march of the human spirit—unfortunately still caught up in the 'Eurocentrism' of Hegel—Husserl showed the way. Blending Hegel and Husserl, bringing in our knowledge of Oriental and African experi-ences, I thought I could write a new *Phenomenology*.

IV

I have come a long way from my Presidency College student years. I have earlier noted how my thinking became theoretical, and early politi-cal and eschatological interests were left behind. Now almost thirty years later, the sense for the *practical* has, virtually ignored earlier, returned. My Göttingen teacher Josef König's distinction between the theoretical and the practical, so long in abeyance in my thinking, surfaced some time in the eighties. Hanah Arendt's writings reinforced a Gandhian sense for the *political*. Much of my efforts were spent in trying to draw a clear distinction between 'theory' and 'practice'—a distinction I hope will go into the structure of my revised Phenomenology. I have now a renewed sense of the importance of the ethical and the political. The Hindu concept of *dharma*, which I had so long expelled from my thinking, now

occupies a central position. And if I can have another decade for thinking, this will be the focal point of my investigations.

What a wonderful and exhilarating path it has been! A journey which
is almost entirely within the interiority of my life of thinking. The
publications mark milestones, determined by external and contingent
circumstances. Shielded from public view, the life of the mind is most
rewarding, especially when it has been able to replace religion. Religion, with its thick layers of beliefs and dogmas, has become meaning-
less for me. It survives only as a thin layer of the sense for the sacredness
of nature, life and persons, and also as a layer of practices—rituals and
dharma—which, for me, is the Hegelian *Sittlichkeit*, a tradition outside
of which I have no place to stand. With religion reduced to irrelevance,
the life of philosophical thinking has replaced it and gained autonomy.
A philosopher *needs* to be an atheist but with a sensitivity to the
sacredness all around. Only if there is no God, will thinking and acting
gain the full significance they demand.

V

The philosopher is still a concrete human being: however far-flung and
cosmic his thinking may be; the thinker is still an embodied, historically
situated, biologically constituted, socially rooted, linguistically local-
ized and culturally conditioned creature. It is a miracle that he can use
these constraints to open out, in his thoughts, to the world at large.

I am an Oriya, I was born in Cuttack. My father was a village boy. My
village roots are indelibly printed in my being. The features of that village—its soil, its trees, its ponds, its greenery, its temples, its cattle—speak
to me in a language I understand. My two mothers are—the village, and
the one from whose womb I emerged into the light. These two 'origins'
are the constituents of my being. And yet, none of my philosophy is
focused on them. After giving birth to me, they let me be free to wander
around the world. I do not know my own DNA, my own *karmic*
inheritance but my thinking moves unrestricted. My origin and inheritance set me free.

At the age of seventeen, I migrated to Bengal, uprooted from my
native soil. How could I take root there? I picked up the language, made
friends, and flourished. The new roots again set me free. The original
roots remained in memory. Memory sought to reach back. What it
recovers are traces of the past. When I go to my village, those traces
cling to every aspect of it. But my present was being constituted
elsewhere, i.e., in Calcutta.

A radical transplantation took place when I moved to Germany, and then years later to the USA. The German language and German philosophy became parts of my being. I thought through them. No such 'taking roots', however, occurred in America. You bring your roots, branches to America, and you live with them—a little transformed and transmitted. You still remain a rootless individual.

Thus, there are layers of rootedness, to all of which I cling with utmost tenacity. Yet in my thinking, I wish to be free. The ability to think with a conceptuality which transcends traditions—in my case, Indian, German, and American—amazes me. A tradition nourishes your life, makes possible a meaningful world but leaves openings through which other traditions may be contacted. No tradition is a closed windowless monad.

I am not merely an Oriya, I am also an Indian. I am also a human, with the entire history of human consciousness shaping me. In this way I realize I am the midpoint of a series of concentric circles. To actualize those circles within my consciousness is what it takes to be a world-philosopher. Dialogue with other traditions is also a dialogue within oneself.

VI.

In the course of my philosophical journey, and in the process of recovering my roots, it is not unusual for me to try to ascertain what has happened to my religious beliefs. It must already have been clear to my readers that I have lost most of them—while, I must add, preserving a core of what I call 'religiosity'. The important thing about a life's story is not so much where the story ends but the path it has followed. So let me reconstruct that path so far as religion is concerned.

I was born into a deeply religious family, where life moved around the family temple. Raised amongst Vaisnava practices, I imbibed the love for Krishna's life, and learned to sing songs in praise of the lord. When in the village, there would be non-stop (*akhanda*) singing, by the community, in Krishna's praise and in chanting his names, sometimes for twenty-four hours, sometimes for days together. Those were highly emotional experiences—along with all the dancing and singing it involved—for a twelve-year-old boy, who never gave up the hope of sometimes having a vision of the Divine one. That good fortune never occurred for me. Since my father did not quite believe in the priestly privileges of the *Brahmins*, he encouraged me to do the rituals for Lord Jagannath, who was the centre of the puja room of the family. I enjoyed doing the *ārati*, which involved amongst other things, delicately and gracefully moving the lamp-holder before the idols. The way my father was moved by the rituals became a part of my appreciation of religious life.

At fifteen, under the influence of Sri Aurobindo's ideas, I thought of myself as beginning to practise yogic meditation. My early immersion in Vaisnava rituals became less important, although they still continued to bring tears to my eyes and choke my throat with emotion. What Aurobindo's writings made me believe is that by practising meditation, I could let a cosmic spirit descend into my being, take hold of me, and use my resources for a cosmic transformation. The idea squared well with my Gandhian obsession to save and uplift humankind. Aurobindo convinced me that politics and religion, the service of humankind and the yogic pursuit of spirituality, could and should go together. The possibility of a new religion which accommodates social and political reforms was brought home by Gandhi. My new search was for a religion which could bring Gandhi and Aurobindo together. Yoga and social/ political activism were inseparable—did not Vivekananda stand for that as well? The religious point of view was strengthened, now freed from Vaisnava ritualism, and provided a rock from which Marxism could be challenged and defeated.

This renewed confidence in the political implication of religion centred in yoga found its decisive end during the 'Great Calcutta Killings' during my B.A. final year—also the last year of British rule in India. After having lived through a carnage, in which Hindus and Muslims killed each other in thousands, I asked myself what the value of religion was, and in whose name, over the centuries, and now before my eyes, could such acts of wanton cruelty be perpetrated? Gandhi's path was to inculcate true religion, which breeds mutual respect and tolerance. I would run, when the Mahatma was in the city, to his prayer meetings, where recitations from all the major religions were read. It did inspire but I thought otherwise. Might it not be more effective if the importance of religion in my life were totally de-emphasized?

When I accompanied Vinoba in his *padayātrā*, he would talk about *bhaktimārga*, the path of devotion, of the Maharashtra saints; his eyes would be full of tears as he spoke about Tukaram and Jnaneswar, and also of Kabir. Again, I witnessed an attempt to bring about social change with the help of religion. Vinoba often used the plain believer's language. When the first landlord in Telengana came up to him with a gift of land, he saw God's presence in him. Such locutions stirred something within me but soon left me cold, whereas the progress of the land-gift movement, or attending to Gandhian *sarvodaya* conference would inspire me with a new vision of both end and means. What had that to do with religion? Vinoba would often, in his more intellectual moments, de-emphasize the word 'religion' and prefer to speak of the necessity of reconciling science with self-knowledge—*vijñāna* with *ātmajñāna*? Spirituality, not religion, he would say, is what is needed in the age of modern science and nuclear weapons. What was 'spirituality'?

Again, my mind would go back to the figures whom I adored as symbols of spirituality: Sri Ramakrishna, Vivekananda, Gandhi, Auro-bindo, Tagore; also Krishna Prem, and Ramana Maharshi. But did they not all still speak the language of religion, of 'God', the 'Divine'? Could I entirely reject the language of religion, and consequently the associ-ated beliefs, and yet pin my faith in the idea of spirituality? That was my last resort. By the end of the eighties I had been able to do that.

In between, lay the experience of witnessing my mother's struggle with her religion. Sometime in the seventies—I had returned to India from the US—she asked me if it was good for her to take initiation or *dīkṣā* from a guru. I was surprised that she should ask me such a question. But in order that my scepticism did not mar her faith, I took her to Tara Chatterjee's father, who was supposed to have some insight into these matters. The old man talked to her for several hours, at the end of which she had made up her mind. She went back to Orissa and took *dīkṣā* from a local holy man, Baya Baba (the crazy one). She would after that spend a lot of time in this person's ashram, and found comfort in his guidance. I was happy. The guru passed away sometime in the early years of the eighties, and she felt abandoned, for she had hoped she would be able to meet her own death with fortitude with his spiritual guidance. Left alone again, she would talk to me openly. Towards the end, she once, much to my surprise, said to me, 'I am grateful to you for having made it possible for me to take initiation. Now, I am ready to go.' And she died in peace, when the evening service in the family temple was being performed along with all the attendant music. As she passed away, my need—whatever need I felt—for religion was over.

I was much clearer than ever before in my mind that I did not believe in God. Why not say that to the world—'*śṛnavantu sarve*' at the top of my voice? I declared myself to be a 'semantic agnostic'. I did not even quite understand what 'God' meant. 'Don't you believe in some power?', friends asked. Of course, I did believe in many different things. Why should any of the things I believed in be called 'God', if, indeed, it was not God but something else? I have more sympathy and understanding of what the Upaniṣads call the *brahman*, but it was muddle-headed to say the *brahman* is God.

Once I clearly and unambiguously rejected belief in God, the idea of *spirituality*, despite its equivocations and ambiguities, became more interesting. Philosophy, as a search for the transcendental ground of mundanity, began to make sense. I also attempted to recover the sense of religiosity that was important for me. Religiosity now meant to me a sensitivity to the irreducible sacredness of things: the sacredness of life, sacredness of humanity, and sacredness of nature; the moral responsibility to preserve life, nature and humankind, to let humans flourish and develop to their best ability—in brief, using Whitehead's expression, 'world-loyalty'.

I do not deny God's existence because I hold a materialistic world view that matter is all that there is. On the contrary, I totally reject materialism as a bad philosophy. Idealism, for me is a quite plausible philosophy. But all these issues have nothing to do with the question of God's existence. The point is, we neither understand what 'God' means, nor have I ever understood what human need the alleged 'God' fulfils. Conventional religious belief impedes both thinking and action.

Freed from that burden, I feel free to think. Thinking is hard; to follow the path of thinking is harder still. To fall while moving along this path is the best good fortune that a thinker can hope for. Can I have the good fortune, in this regard, of my dear friend Hannah Arendt?

American Life in the Last
Three Decades

When I arrived in the United States of America for the first time, the Vietnam War was in full swing, and I watched President Johnson vow on the television to carry on the battle until the Communists were defeated. When I returned, two years later, student protest against the war was at its height. I was taken aback when a graduate student expressed his surprise that I should have emigrated to the USA at a time when the country had lost all moral greatness as never before. Students at Stanford burnt a campus building (the well-known Indian sociologist M.N. Srinivas lost his research notes in that fire). In Columbia University, the students took over the administration building. In Norman, the Vietnam flag was hoisted on the campus. At Kent State in Ohio, several students died from the National Guard gunfire. The campuses seemed to be on fire. Political unrest bred spiritual hunger. Both political authority and the church came under cloud of suspicion—culminating in the Hippie movement, the Woodstock music festival, the proliferation of eastern spiritual seekers (and, correlatively, gurus), the use of drugs such as marijuana for raising one's consciousness, free sex, and overall, the search for a new brand of spirituality. My Indian philosophy classes at the New School started off by being over-crowded but ended up with half a dozen students as the discussions became more and more discursive, and less and less to do with 'consciousness raising'. It is amazing how a political error of Kennedy and Johnson brought about the massive transformation of the life and culture of the young. A new idealism, an intense longing for something new and ennobling—for something whose absence was lamented by my student David Power—emerged.

As I look back, after thirty years, to those Vietnam War days, what a

sea change I notice in the life and ideals in the USA! The milestones in
the political arena were: the assassination of the Kennedy brothers and
of Martin Luther King (with whom I had dined in Calcutta), the eventual
defeat and withdrawal of American troops from Vietnam; the Watergate
scandal and President Nixon's resignation to avoid impeachment (I
watched Nixon leave the White House on the television), and the
emergence of the Reagan era, marked by a new culture of greed, self-
aggrandizement, attempts to set the clock back as far as civil rights,
affirmative action, and anti-poverty programmes were concerned. Coming to more recent times, I must mention the new Republican majority in
the House. Newt Gingrich's 'Contract with America' embodying the
ideal of the pursuit of self-interest (a la Ayn Rand), hoping that this will
benefit all in the long run, Rush Limbaugh's deliberate attempt to
transform, in the public eye, the feminist movement from having brought
about awareness (as well as social change) of women's rights, into a
'feminazi' movement, with its attendant 'Nazi-like' tactics; and the
consequent critique of 'liberalism' as the irresponsible, self-serving
ideology of the intellectually elite. What a change from the time when to
be a liberal was regarded as being noble of character and concerned
about removing poverty and the evils of racism! Now, in the nineties,
the liberal 'bleeding heart' intellectual is abused, and the conservative,
engaged in pursuing self interest, is praised. 'Welfare' is today regarded
as corrupting its recipients, perpetuating and imprisoning them in their
poverty. If in the early eighties, the 'Reagan democrats' were young
democrats opting for Reaganite economic reforms (converted to 'supply-
side economics' and cutting down taxes for the wealthy), today the
Clintonite democrats (and also the Tony Blair-led labourites) are regarded as having 'hijacked' the Republican programmes of cutting
down the welfare budget. A middle-of-the-road political economy has
come to prevail as the century comes to a close.

The breakdown of the Soviet empire brought about the demise of
European communism, and the Chinese communists are eager to accommodate capitalist economy. Ideologies are ceasing to be world
forces, and oppositions between ideologies are softening. In the United
States, one still hears of the reigning ideology, i.e., 'Free-market
economy'. But one does not realize that the free market that reigns today
is different from Adam Smith's. Three factors make for that difference:
there is a great deal of government regulation to promote public good, or
at least to ward off public danger; the huge government-owned defence
and armament production, even if contracted out to private contractors,
is ruled by, and marketed to, the state; and, finally millions of ordinary

citizens buying stocks through mutual funds share in the ownership of companies. The fact is that new technology makes the old dominance of ideologies—be it socialism or free market, pointless. A new society, which we do not quite understand, seems to be on the horizon.

It is precisely in this complex situation that I find myself losing my way. When I left India thirty years ago, I could say with relative certainty that I was a Gandhian socialist (not a state-socialist). The word 'capitalism'—as I grew up in India—had for us pejorative connotations: a capitalist was taken to be a ruthlessly selfish person who appropriated all profits for himself at the cost of the hard labour of the impoverished and de-humanized workers. The word 'socialism' correspondingly had benign, even ethically praiseworthy connotations (despite the ruthlessness associated with the Stalinist regime). If you live in the United States, the connotations would be reversed for you: 'socialism' would mean something despicable, the ruthless denial of individual freedom, while the capitalist would be regarded as one who, by his self-aggrandizement, created jobs for others, who is a symbol of free enterprise, initiative and human potentiality.

Many Indian friends in the USA—doctors, scientists, and technologists—have imbibed this new reversal of meanings. It is not that you arrive at this changed significance by your own thinking. It is rather the over-powerful media (including the *Wall Street Journal*) which foster the comfortable self-satisfaction that you know the truth. Why else should you be so wealthy and powerful, and why should socialist Russia have collapsed? I have tried, in conversations, to argue that these examples do not prove the case; that, as a matter of fact, in American life there is not mere selfish pursuit but, on the contrary, there is a great deal of social sense, caring for others, altruism, and a sense of community, and that if Russia collapsed, that is not because of an inner deficiency of socialism but because of the ruthless imperialism of the Stalinist–Leninist dictatorship.

Several important truths seem to have escaped the point of view fostered by the American media. Individual freedom is not selfishness; pursuit of unmitigated self-interest is not the height of that freedom. Social order is not simply an aggregate of individuals, each pursuing his own self-interest, but requires that these freely acting agents be permeated by a social sense that is not authoritatively imposed but is spontaneously enjoyed. In no case could selfishness be the highest of human virtues. Altruism, self-sacrifice, and benevolence have to be accorded that place. American society exhibits all these, while the theory which is posited as undergirding it tells a different story. But that theory appears to be working only because of the pervasive altruistic spirit that imperceptibly permeates life.

Gandhi still seems to have a relevance. Unlimited greed must be self-defeating, as Plato knew twenty-five centuries ago. Communitarianism seems to provide a third alternative to capitalism and socialism, and information technology seems to favour the Gandhian ideal of a decentralized economy.

Keeping a Promise

I had promised my mother that I would consign her ashes to the Ganges, and perform the necessary rituals at Gaya. Every Hindu wants the rituals to be preformed after he or she is gone. Nine years had passed since she died, and I was still hoping to keep my promise. When my eldest brother died, and my own health began declining, the urgency of visiting Gaya took hold of me, and I made up my mind. But could I make the trip—about a twelve-hour train journey from Calcutta—and go through the trials and tribulations of the elaborate priestly ceremonies, all by myself? Given the state of her health, Bani could not accompany me. It was at this time that Bina Gupta and her husband, Madan, came to my aid.

But let me first explain why a person who is a self-proclaimed atheist, a western-trained analytic thinker, and one who has lived in the West for thirty years, be so intent on performing the rituals in Gaya, which involve offering oblations to the departed souls. Have I not said earlier in this narrative that I do not believe in after-life? And so I do not believe that my parents have another existence after they departed. My determination to make the trip to Gaya and perform the rituals, was due to two considerations: first, I must keep my promise to my mother, and the obligation to keep my promise does not depend on her watching me from above. Like Pascal, I argued, if she is not there, that should not make me to go back on my word; and in case my belief is wrong, and she is there watching me, my keeping my promise would please her, and perhaps in some sense 'save' her from 'rebirth'. In any case, I ought to take the trouble to go to Gaya.

Philosophically, although I no longer subscribe to implied metaphysical beliefs, I still believe that performing 'rituals' is obligatory. In this mode of thinking, I am as much influenced by the Mīmāṃsā thinkers as by Confucius. The fundamental insight that binds members of a community, inheritors of a tradition, is not so much sharing theoretical beliefs as participating in common social practices (which include ceremonies and rituals). The theoretical self-interpretation of participants may, as a matter of fact, differ, but the fact of participation is what ties the members together in a shared social structure. So even though I am an atheist, I enthusiastically take part in the *pujas*, religious ceremonies and rituals. They attract me as signifying my belongingness to the Hindu tradition, while I do not share all the Hindu beliefs.

So on a winter evening, accompanied by Bina and Madan Gupta, I boarded the train at the Howrah station which would take us to Gaya. All the travel arrangements had been made by Bina. When I left the Rama-krishna Mission for the railway station, I already had fever; my body was hot, and a cough had turned into a non-stop hiccup. The train was several hours late in leaving the station. Waiting in that condition on the platform was uncomfortable. Bina wrapped my head in a blanket, and let me rest inside the car which had taken us there. After a night's train journey, we got down at Gaya station. I was shivering due to the fever. We drove to a hotel in Bodh Gaya, and I was put to bed to rest, half asleep, still hiccuping without pause. In the morning we were to go to the temple where the rituals were to be performed.

Bodh Gaya is the place where Guatama attained enlightenment and became the Buddha. The thought of being there was exhilarating but I was shivering with fever. As we went from Bodh Gaya to Gaya in a rikhshaw, a distance of about six miles, we followed the banks of the river Falgu. It did not escape me that after attaining his wisdom, this was the path on which Gautama Siddhartha walked, along the river Falgu, up to Benaras, where he preached his first sermon. The hills on both sides, that I now saw, were certainly there at the time of the Buddha, but not the same trees and bushes. The river bed must be wider now than it was then, so the grass his feet trod upon must be now in the riverbed. We know that people from neighbouring villages flocked to see this young holy man. My imagination wandered freely across two and a half millennia. Did he pass through Gaya? How did the priestly tradition in Gaya respond to him?

Before going further in my narrative, a few words about Bina, who became my friend and saviour. Her family hailed from Ambala, in the Punjab, but Bina was born and raised in Calcutta. Eventually, she came to Santiniketan to study philosophy. It was then that she attended some of my classes. But I really met her in the USA, when she joined one of my summer seminars sponsored by the National Endowment for the

Humanities. She had already started teaching at the University of Missouri. When I got to know her next, nearly fifteen years later, she was already a full professor and had published a work on the Advaita Vedanta theory of perception, and was thinking about writing on the concept of *sākṣī-caitanya* or witness-consciousness. This book was about to appear, when she offered to accompany me to Gaya. An accomplished Vedanta scholar, she continues to help me in preparing my manuscripts, and for the last few years all my manuscripts have passed through her careful hands. Now I feel as if without her help I cannot write anything for the press! She has sacrificed her own time for doing creative work—although she is engaged in several research projects—for my sake.

With high fever, an unceasing hiccup, with a *dhoti* and a shawl, I stood in the temple, where a priest exempted me from dipping my feet in the river, and I followed him reciting all the Sanskrit *ślokas*. I tried to focus on the Sanskrit verses, hymns and prayers, grasp their meanings (which was not too difficult for me), tried to situate myself in the cosmic order in which they make sense. I did not have much difficulty in praying for my ancestors, for my parents, and three brothers who are no more. I was exhilarated when I realized that the priest made me pray for all the dead anywhere in the world, for those who have none to pray for them, for those who, as the verse ran, 'were eaten by tigers in the forest, who had killed themselves (and so were not entitled to the oblations), who died of snake-bite, who died leaving no one to mourn them', and so on and so on. I felt that having come to pray for my mother, I was indeed praying for all the departed, and wondered if there was any difference between the two prayers!

With the rituals over, we returned to the hotel. My hiccups were getting more frequent and my chest and ribs were sore. Bina hurried to a doctor in the town, who gave me a strong sedative. I fell into a deep sleep. Later in the night they transported me in a rickshaw to the railway station, as I vaguely recall. The train for Calcutta was ten hours late, it was bitter cold, and the station's platform was so crowded that there was hardly any place to stand or sit, and I was heavily sedated. I have only a faint recollection of when we boarded the train. Waking up late around noon, I found myself sleeping on a berth on the train, hiccups over, and the fever gone. Tired but relaxed, I recollected the events of the past two days, and wondered if it had been a dream. Getting down in Calcutta, we asked the driver—Bina had arranged for her sister-in-law's car—to take us to the RKMI. I had hardly eaten anything during the last two days; Bina suggested that we finish our work before we went anywhere to get a bite to eat. So we first went to a *ghat* of the Ganges. I steadily walked down the broad steps of the *ghat*, into the water, and emptied my mother's ashes into the brown waters of the holy river.

Back at the Ramakrishna Mission, I felt as light and luminous as I have seldom felt before. But I recalled—for the first time—that fifteen years ago, when we were spending the summer in Calcutta near Lake Market, my mother came to live with us when I was down with fever and had an uncontrollable bout of hiccups, which continued for almost twenty-four hours, even while sleeping. Bani said, 'Mother was sitting beside you all through the night.' This time I had gone in search of her spirit. Could she have been there in Gaya? It felt spooky to think about it. Bina filled the void left by my mother's death.

All this coincided with my turning seventy later that year. In an international conference sponsored by the Society for Asian and Comparative Philosophy and Utkal University in Bhubaneswar, the present President of the society, Bina Gupta, presented me with a leather-bound volume of letters she had solicited from colleagues, friends, and students in a rather moving ceremony. It touched me more than it ordinarily would have, because the reception was held in Orissa, was attended by close friends from the West, as well as by members of my family. The Vice-Chancellor of Utkal University joined in, presenting me with a plaque. Wasn't I one of their former students?

This story ends with the year 1998.

Epilogue

Swami Lokeswaranda died, and I had to move my Calcutta home from the Ramakrishna Mission Institute of Culture elsewhere. We bought a flat in Calcutta; I spent two nights there to satisfy the requirements of the puja performed for entering a home. An extraordinary cyclone had hit the Orissa coast, destroying, amongst others, most of my village. My elder sister passed away, and, for a few days before the end, constantly talked about her brother, the philosopher. Bani's arthritis is getting worse, I have to help her in her daily chores. Bina tirelessly carries on her editorial work.

The large Husserl book on which I have been working is yet to be written. With the help of Bina, however, several books, most of them on Indian philosophy, but some on phenomenology, are about to be published. Bina is also editing a *Festschrift* for me, which she has titled, *The Empirical and the Transcendental: A Fusion of Horizons*.

It has been an exhilarating life, about which I have no complaints. I either did not do or did not succeeded in doing everything that, as a young man, I had dreamt of. Amongst those dreams are: doing Gandhian village-level social work, political activism, practising *yoga*. Instead, I have spent a life devoted to thinking, with few outer manifestations. The books written are not results of thinking, but mark different phases in that process. That process is its own reward.

Living outside India has been hard—comfortable for my outer life, but hard for my inner one. The choice deprived me of many sources of emotional enrichment. But spending a lifetime in a country of adoption is also rewarding. In America, you become a part of a vibrant intellectual life. To combine the rich philosophical heritage of India with the ever-awake intellectual life of America is a benefit which one reaps. Only, one should not be misled into thinking of America—under pressure of power—as the centre of the universe. There are as many centres as there are human communities. My village, now in ruins, is one.

Life is incomplete, and as Heidegger puts it, is being-towards-death. However, Heidegger misconstrues the nature of human existence by his one-sided description. There is, in the midst of this constant self-exceeding, a fixed point of self-reference which Husserl captured in his concept of transcendental ego. This prevents self-dissipation, a pointless scattering in outward-directed projects. The process of living, with its ever-new projects, always tends to return to that centre, where they are unified.

This life will be complete, in its incompleteness, with my death. Then it will be a matter for judgment by others. The fundamental question for judgment, will be: 'What was the point of it all', not the simple moral question, 'Was he a good or a bad person?' For myself, living this life has been, if successful, an aesthetic project. Has it been enjoyable, harmonious, and fulfilling?

15 October 2000

Appendix:
My Contribution to Philosophy

It is most probably Heidegger who remarked that every philosopher has one central *problem* which he is concerned with in all perspectives, at different depths, and with many variations—as happens with a musical theme.

Besides such a central problem, I should add, a philosopher also wrestles with certain texts, or certain figures, which beckon him all through his life.

The problem which captured my imagination early in my thinking life is what may be called the problem of Platonism. Are there entities which are Platonic, ideal entities as the Germans called them, abstract entities as the logicians named them? I was convinced that there are. Much of my early work—including my Göttingen dissertation—consisted in showing that nominalistic denials of such entities will not do. I soon began to realize that what is brought under the title of Platonism is a whole array of diverse entities; essences and meanings to introduce a preliminary division of that realm. Once this ontology is rehabilitated, one confronts several questions: is psychologistic reduction (psychologism) any more viable than the nominalistic? Even if psychologism is rejected, how does the mind apprehend or group these entities? These questions are alive, and I seek to understand and answer them in my most recent writings on phenomenology—after nearly four decades. It is these questions which connect Husserl and Frege in my thoughts. I found in these questions a central point from where I mediate between analytic philosophy and continental philosophy: here the issues cluster around a satisfactory theory of meaning. Reductionist psychologism had, no doubt, to be rejected but the mental and ideal meanings had to be bonded together, which required a new concept of the mental as a correlation between two strata—real acts and ideal meanings.

Long before my research into phenomenology took shape, I had embarked on the study of Navya-Nyāya epistemology, which resulted in *Gangeśa's Theory of Truth*. I also studied the major Vedantic texts, which resulted in my writings on Indian philosophy during the last few years. *Gangeśa's Theory of Truth* contained an English translation of Gangeś's chapter on knowledge of truth and also a detailed analysis of the problems and arguments surrounding the concept of *prāmāṇya*. The original contribution of this book to philosophy is not much. Its service is by way of expounding the doctrines of Navya-Nyāya, commenting on the texts in a manner that is faithful to the work and the method of the Pandit tradition, and to present the theories of the various schools on *prāmāṇya* in an analytical manner. Translation of some other chapters from the '*Pratyakṣakhanda*' of *Tattvachintāmaṇi* are unfished, and hopefully will be completed before long.

In the papers on Indian philosophy, which I have published during the last thirty years or so, I have been concerned with the nature of Indian logic, the theory of meaning, issues surrounding the realism-idealism debate, the nature of the *pramāṇa* theories, the idea of reducibility of *śabda* as a *pramāṇa*, and the claim of *śruti* to be *apauruṣeya*. The studies and the resulting theses were brought together in *Reason and Tradition in Indian Philosophy*. Besides giving new interpretations of old concepts and theories (e.g., a theory of quasi-*Sinn* ascribed to the Navya-Nyāya account of meaning), I have, in this book, pleaded for the recognition of the claims of memory, history and mathematics to be irreducible types of valid cognition. A continuation of these researches into the domains of action-theory, freedom and art is being completed. The connecting link between the two areas is provided by a series of lectures given in Calcutta in 1992, and published under the title *Theory and Practice*, and in a couple of journal articles on the theme 'Theory and Practice in Indian Thought'. In these publications, I have insisted on the purely theoretical character of a large segment of Indian thought, also ascribed to it a theory of action and practice, and have argued that the ideal of *mokṣa* espoused in the different *darśanas* is heavily clouded by the theoretical concepts of the system concerned.

In some of the papers of the last five years, I have drawn attention to some very interesting and tantalizing features of the dialectic of knowledge and ignorance in Advaita Vedanta, to the unsatisfactoriness of Samkara's criticisms of Buddhist philosophies, and to the many ways

Vedanta has been understood, interpreted, and appropriated in modern Indian thought.

Besides my continuing engagement with the task of interpreting Husserl's phenomenology (in the light of his total corpus including the *Nachlass*), I have also undertaken a reformulation and defence of transcendental philosophy in the tradition of Kant, Hegel, and Husserl. According to my reformulation, transcendental subjectivity (in whose life all meanings have their origin) is historical (here I am indebted to Hegel's *Phenomenology of the Mind*), corporeal and linguistic (I owe to insights from Husserl), as well as inter-subjective (following Merleau-Ponty). I have also sought to respond to the criticisms of transcendental philosophy by de-constructionists such as Derrida and historicists such as Foucault.

However, in this process of dialogue with the post-modernists, I have also appropriated into my own thinking some of their important insights—most importantly, the reduction of identities to systems of differences. Thus I have spoken of 'layers of selfhood' instead of a fixed identity, and of cultural identities as reducible to systems of differences—as a consequence of which the concepts of cultural relativism and incommensurability amongst radically different cultures become deceptively spurious. First representing cultures as circles (á la Herder), I defended the possibility of intercultural understanding with the idea of intersecting circles. Then, I reflected on that representation of a culture as a circle and defended the thesis that a cultural unity is a construct out of 'systems of differences'. The distinction between 'intercultural' and 'intracultural' thereby gets blurred; we have then to adopt, in the words of Welsch, the standpoint of 'transculturality'. These ideas have been for the first time expounded in my Calcutta lectures during the last five years. These lectures have been put together in *The Self and Its Other*, just published by the Oxford University Press, Delhi.

The path of thinking has not been solipsistic. Many students, colleagues and friends in India have contributed to it: so also have innumerable friends in the USA and Germany. The responsibility for the positions I have taken is, however, always mine, and the path is still open-ended. Thinking cannot have a closure.

Glossary

āddā	free, endless conversation
ārati	worshipping a deity with a lamp
ashrama	the centre of a holy person
avidyā	ignorance
bhajan	(usually collective) singing of devotional songs
bou	the author called his mother 'bou'
brahmacārin	the practitioner of the path of brahman
dīkṣā	initiation
dhoti	a garment of Indians
ghāt	the steps from the bank leading to the water of a river
golapbag	garden of roses
guru	teacher
Kṛṣṇa	an incarnation of Visnu
māyā	illusion
puja	religious ritual of worship, usually a deity
punjabi	a kind of shirt worn by many Indians
pramāṇa	Means of true cognition
śabdapramāṇa	'word' as a means of true cognition
sāl-bithi	promenade of 'sāl' trees
sarvodaya	'flourishing of all', the economic and social utopia conceived by Mahatma Gandhi
Tāntric	pertaining to the Hindu sect 'Tantra'
zamindari	landlordhship